EDIBLE BROOKLYN: THE COOKBOOK

EDIBLE BROOKLYN: THE COOKBOOK

EDITED BY RACHEL WHARTON

PHOTOGRAPHS BY CAROLE TOPALIAN

STERLING EPICURE

New York

STERLING EPICURE
New York

An Imprint of Sterling Publishing
387 Park Avenue South
New York, NY 10016

Distributed in Canada by Sterling Publishing
c/o Canadian Manda Group, 165 Dufferin Street
Toronto, Ontario, Canada M6K 3H6

For information about custom editions, special sales, and premium and corporate purchases,
please contact Sterling Special Sales at 800-805-5489 or specialsales@sterlingpublishing.com.

Manufactured in the United States of America

2 4 6 8 10 9 7 5 3 1

www.sterlingpublishing.com

Contents

FOREWORD

What you hold in your hands is the first in a new generation of community cookbooks.

It's thoroughly cutting-edge—gleaned from the kitchens and pantries of the chefs, drink makers, old-school costermongers, rooftop gardeners, avid eaters, and the entire motley crew that makes up today's Brooklyn food community. But *Edible Brooklyn: The Cookbook* is also an old soul—kin to the community cookbooks that have been published by churches, schools, and other collections of like-minded individuals throughout North America for centuries.

Communities crave cookbooks. In fact, they need them—to document and codify food traditions; to remind us of what's in season; to chronicle and celebrate the people in our communities who feed and sustain us. No matter if today's cookbook is organized by urban CSA members or the teachers behind an edible schoolyard project. Or if recipes once gathered on ruled cards are now crowd-sourced on e-mail. The mission remains the same.

This same mission was part inspiration for *Edible Ojai*, the first Edible magazine, launched in 2002. The simple and revolutionary idea—which has now manifested in nearly seventy Edible magazines in big cities, little towns, and everywhere in between—was that telling the story behind our food would encourage us all to eat better, restore our landscape, support our neighbors, and generally make food and drink experiences a bigger, richer part of our collective lives.

Beginning with Brooklyn, and following with Seattle, Dallas–Forth Worth, the Twin Cities, and beyond, Edible Communities, the network of local food magazines in distinct culinary regions throughout the United States and Canada, will publish a series of cookbooks that celebrate those areas where Edible magazines exist. In keeping with the pages of local Edible magazines, these cookbooks invite one hundred or so people from the various food communities to submit original recipes that tell something about their place—and their place in it.

This particular installation is jam-packed with such dishes as the beer-chicken creation from the founder of one of the nation's largest craft breweries; the chili from a top NPR host, spiced with the Mexican peppers now found throughout Brooklyn; an off-cut meat dish from the director of the city's Greenmarkets; and a simple cheese and pickle sandwich from a pioneer of American farmstead cheesemongering. Regional concentrations of DIYers may vary, but in this age of acronyms, we're confident that what's cooking in Brooklyn offers a glimpse of what's happening well beyond the borders of New York City.

Wherever you may be, please consider this cookbook inspiration to get to know the people who feed you.

—*Tracey Ryder, co-founder, Edible Communities;*
Brian Halweil and Stephen Munshin, publishers,
Edible Brooklyn

BROOKLYN FARMACY, COBBLE HILL

INTRODUCTION

We have to admit we feel a bit smug, living and eating in Brooklyn, which is technically not a city or a town but a borough, one of five that make up the great city of New York. That's partly because of our size and our historical status: with 2.5 million diners—um, people—we occupy the second-largest county in the country, one appropriately called Kings. Our "beautiful hills," as native Walt Whitman so wonderfully put it in "Crossing Brooklyn Ferry," part of his 1900 masterpiece *Leaves of Grass*, were first hunted, foraged, and fished by the Lenape Indians and later farmed and colonized by the Dutch as early as 1646—except back then they called it Breuckelen.

But the real reason for our self-satisfaction is that we feel pretty certain there is no better place to live and to eat in the country, especially right now: Berkeley may have the ability to grow lemons; New Orleans has gumbo; but Brooklyn, well, we have pretty much everything else.

Urban farm-gardens and incredible markets loaded with rarely seen greens and pristine pasture-raised meats? In fact, farming has precedent here: we grew almost all our own food up until the 1900s. A waterfront where bluefish and herring run and boats still depart for the big catch? That too, though we don't see the mammoth oysters our Dutch forebears used to.

CSA pickups on every other street? Secret raw-milk clubs, kombucha by the pint, pickles by the gallon, the East Coast's most successful independent food co-op, and pale blue and brown eggs from backyard co-ops and community gardens for four dollars a dozen? Yes—plus some of the nation's best cheesemongers, butchers, bakers, brewers, chocolatiers, wine sellers, cocktail bars, beer gardens, and even our own mini booze boom: in 2010, three tiny distilleries opened their doors right here. Not to mention chefs with Michelin stars, restaurants with sky-high Zagat Survey rankings, and food artisans featured constantly in the glossy pages of national food magazines.

And that's just the cutting edge of the blade that makes up modern Brooklyn food. Name nearly any food culture and there's a community living it within our borders, not to mention shopping at the most amazing Ukrainian/Vietnamese/Trinidadian/fill-in-the-blank market you've ever seen. We have our own Chinatown; a strip where tamale makers share street corners with Salvadoran snack shops; the largest Caribbean population outside of the West Indies; a Middle Eastern grocery row; a Little Odessa by the Atlantic Ocean; a Little Poland up near Queens; and let's not forget soul food, Jewish delis, fresh mozzarella and meatball makers, Junior's cheesecake, and last but not least, the steaks at Peter Luger's.

So how do we begin to tell the story of Brooklyn food? Through our eaters, naturally. This is not a tome of famous historical foods like Ebinger's Brooklyn Blackout Cake, or a report from the best of Brooklyn's new chefs. This is instead a crowd-sourced collective from our rooftop farmers and sauerkraut picklers and bonbon makers, including: a musician who writes ditties for our summer ice cream trucks; a third-generation owner of a Lebanese grocery; a community-garden beekeeper originally from Trinidad; and the bartender from one of the borough's hottest restaurants, who makes homemade bitters from the place's backyard trees.

It's not just dishes, in other words, but dozens of stories of how Brooklyn—the home of those beautiful hills and the borough of Kings—lives and cooks and eats.

—*Rachel Wharton*

CHAPTER 1

SMALL PLATES AND SNACKS

Snacks have always been a serious pastime

in Brooklyn—and not just because we're lucky enough to have a superior pizza joint on every corner. Every culture has its fix: Dominican diners with *chicharrones*, Mexican taco trucks, and don't forget the slew of food markets—Italian, Middle Eastern—where you can graze on charcuterie or pickled radishes and spicy olive hummus. Nowadays those have been joined by artisans and cooks elevating the small plate—a triangle of toast smeared with warm puree of white beans or a wedge of fat, olive-oil-soaked focaccia—to a fine art.

ALEXANDER'S OMELET

From Jeff Gorlechen,
Sixpoint Craft Ales

When Jeff Gorlechen cooks—he handles promotions for the small craft brewery he co-owns in the artsy neighborhood of Red Hook, meaning he's often out at beer-pairing dinners around the borough—it's usually for his young son, Alex. Hence this simple but stellar one-egg omelet beefed up with great olive oil, beans, avocados, and a little bit of wheat germ (because, says Gorlechen, "it gives him stuff he would otherwise never get"). Gorlechen apologizes to East Coast cooks for the avocado, which isn't found locally, but we think he makes up for it with his eggs, which are laid by the chickens that live on the brewery's rooftop farm and boast extra-rich, electric orange yolks, thanks to their diet of spent grain. Jeff recommends you pair this with Sixpoint's Righteous Rye (if you're not making it for a child).

Edible Idea

Frank Falcinelli and Frank Castronovo, authors of *The Frankies Spuntino Kitchen Companion and Cooking Manual* and owners of Frankies Spuntino, a modern Italian restaurant near Sixpoint Brewery, import a luscious, very fruity green olive oil that Gorlechen uses to make this omelet. (They sell it at local supermarkets and from *FrankiesSpuntino.com*.)

1   EXTRA-LARGE ORGANIC EGG
1   TBSP ORGANIC WHOLE MILK
1   TBSP ORGANIC WHEAT GERM
SALT
FRESHLY GROUND BLACK PEPPER
1   TSP HIGH-QUALITY EXTRA-
    VIRGIN OLIVE OIL
1   RIPE AVOCADO, 4 TBSP MASHED,
    THE BALANCE CUBED FOR
    GARNISHING

1¼-INCH SLICE COLBY JACK OR
    MILDER CHEDDAR CHEESE,
    PREFERABLY ORGANIC
4   TBSP COOKED AND DRAINED
    BLACK BEANS (CANNED OR
    FRESH)

Makes 1 omelet

1 In a small bowl, beat together the egg, milk, and wheat germ, and season with salt and pepper to taste.

2 Heat the oil in a small, nonstick skillet, making sure that it covers the entire surface of the pan. Pour in the egg mixture, and cook over medium heat for about 3 minutes, or until the egg is cooked on the bottom and no longer runny on top. Do not flip the omelet. Reduce the heat slightly to keep the bottom of the omelet from burning.

3 Spread the mashed avocado across the center of the omelet and top the avocado with the cheese slice. Once the cheese begins to melt, reduce the heat to its lowest setting possible and fold the omelet in half. Leave the omelet in the pan for 30 seconds, and then slide it onto a plate. Keep it warm by covering it with another plate.

4 Heat the black beans in the microwave on medium-high for 30 seconds. Spoon the black beans over the omelet, and let stand for 5 minutes. Garnish with cubed avocado, and season with more salt and pepper to taste.

IAN CHENEY, TRUCK FARMER

In Brooklyn, edible goodness can grow where you'd least expect it.

Back in 2004, Ian Cheney and Curt Ellis took "Old Faithful," the old Dodge Ram pickup Cheney's grandpa gifted him upon his graduation from Yale, on a road trip to the farm country of Iowa, where the pair spent a year toiling on just one acre of soil and filming the results. Their agricultural and artistic collaboration on the impacts of industrial farming became the beloved feature film *King Corn*. But if an acre seems like a tiny patch, it's massive compared to the next plot Cheney would cultivate: the bed of that Dodge Ram, which, along with its owner, settled back east in Brooklyn. (There Cheney and Ellis are currently working on FoodCorps, which will follow the AmeriCorps model to develop farm-to-school food with the help of postcollegiate volunteers.)

In Iowa, it seems, Cheney was bitten by the farming bug. And even though he'd left the open country for concrete, the itch to cultivate kicked in: where would he grow food to eat? The answer, it seems, was parked just outside. As it turned out, the dusty green pickup was one of a number of innovative Brooklyn farming spaces created back in the summer of 2009—from rooftops to run-down barges and borrowed backyards, the borough's hunger for hyperlocal produce had reached a fever pitch, going beyond well-managed community gardens and true urban farms like East New York Farms! and Added Value in the waterfront neighborhood of Red Hook.

But Old Faithful, of course, is the only one that could haul its harvest directly to you by way of the Brooklyn-Queens Expressway. It supplies a tiny CSA; shows up at *Edible Brooklyn* events; is visited by interns from Added Value when parked in Red Hook; stops in at Eagle Street Rooftop Farm in Greenpoint to visit like-minded farmer Annie Novak; and recently scaled the eastern seaboard, making stops at schools along the way to show off its abundance and inspire possibility in eaters everywhere. Best of all, it can always easily pull a U-turn from one side of the street to the other to catch the optimum amount of sun.

BACKYARD EGG TACOS
WITH OVEN-ROASTED SALSA VERDE

From J. Kenji Lopez-Alt,
SeriousEats.com

"My good friend Josh raises chickens Misty and Logan in his Carroll Gardens backyard," says J. Kenji Lopez-Alt, who blogs about recipes and food science for the national website Serious Eats. "Misty and Logan live in a repurposed dresser and have the run of the yard, eating organic feed supplemented with bugs, worms, and flowers. They give Josh about a dozen eggs a week, which he's thankfully very generous with. Simply scrambled and served with some roasted salsa verde, the eggs were the hit of a recent taco party we had." Beyond the goodness of the fresh, local eggs, we imagine it also must've had something to do with his bright and fresh-tasting green salsa, made with the sweet-tart tomatillo, a second cousin to the tomato (and actually in the gooseberry family) that grows with a papery husk and is common in Mexican cooking. If you can't find them in your local supermarket, track them down in a market that carries Mexican products.

Edible Technique

For less heat in your salsa verde, recommends Lopez-Alt, remove the seeds and ribs from the poblanos—the membrane is where chiles really carry their heat—and omit the jalapeño or serrano chile.

1 LB FRESH TOMATILLOS, OUTER HUSKS REMOVED, HALVED
1 MEDIUM ONION, COARSELY CHOPPED (ABOUT ½ CUP)
2 POBLANO CHILES, STEMS REMOVED
1 JALAPEÑO OR SERRANO CHILE, STEM REMOVED, HALVED
4 CLOVES GARLIC
1 TBSP EXTRA-VIRGIN OLIVE OIL
KOSHER SALT
FRESHLY GROUND BLACK PEPPER
1 TBSP FRESH LIME JUICE
2 CUPS CILANTRO LEAVES

1 SMALL RED ONION, SLICED
2 TBSP UNSALTED BUTTER
1 DOZEN FRESH EGGS, LIGHTLY BEATEN
1 PACKAGE TACO-SIZE CORN TORTILLAS, WARMED
1 LIME, CUT INTO 6 WEDGES
¾ CUP *CREMA AGRIA* (MEXICAN SOUR CREAM) OR ¾ CUP SOUR CREAM THINNED WITH 1 TBSP MILK

Serves 6

1 Preheat the broiler. In a large bowl combine the tomatillos and the coarsely chopped onion. Add the poblanos, jalapeño, garlic, and olive oil. Season to taste with salt and pepper, and toss until all vegetables are lightly coated with oil. Spread the vegetables evenly on a heavyweight rimmed baking sheet lined with aluminum foil and broil until they are fully softened and deeply charred, 8–12 minutes.

2 Transfer the vegetables to a food processor along with half the lime juice and 1 cup cilantro leaves. Process until smooth. Adjust seasoning with salt and pepper and additional lime juice as needed. Set aside. Chop the remaining cilantro leaves and toss with the sliced red onion. Set aside.

3 Melt the butter in a large nonstick skillet over medium-low heat. Add the eggs and cook, stirring occasionally with a rubber spatula, until soft curds form. Season the eggs to taste with salt and pepper, and transfer to a large plate when they are softer than you'd like (they will continue to cook off the heat).

4 Serve immediately with warmed tortillas, salsa verde, onions and cilantro, lime wedges, and *crema agria*.

GODFRIED'S ZUCCHINI MUFFINS
WITH HOMEMADE STRAWBERRY BUTTER

From Sandra McClean, founder and chair of Slow Food NYC's Leadership Community, and the children from Slow Food NYC's Urban Harvest program

As part of her work with Slow Food's New York City chapter, Sandra McClean works with the organization's Urban Harvest program, which teaches Brooklyn schoolkids farming skills at a local garden. This recipe was a collaborative effort to cheer up Godfried, a student who ended up in the hospital for a week thanks to a skateboarding accident. Godfried's favorite foods, it seemed, were biscuits and butter, says McClean, so "we brainstormed about how we could put some of our garden into our gift, and came up with the idea that we would make zucchini muffins with strawberry butter. Making butter gave us the opportunity to learn about how a familiar food is made and the zucchini muffins helped us learn about how green can taste great." For those who've never tasted either, this will also be a lesson on how incredibly moist a squash can make a muffin and how incredibly easy homemade butter can be—not to mention how addictive.

FOR THE MUFFINS:
1 CUP SUGAR
2 EGGS, BEATEN
2 TSP VANILLA EXTRACT
3 CUPS GRATED FRESH ZUCCHINI
⅔ CUP MELTED BUTTER
2 TSP BAKING SODA
¼ TSP SALT
3 CUPS ALL-PURPOSE UNBLEACHED FLOUR
1½ TSP GROUND CINNAMON
¼ TSP GRATED NUTMEG
¼ TSP GROUND CLOVES
¼ TSP GROUND GINGER

FOR THE STRAWBERRY BUTTER:
1 CUP STRAWBERRIES, HULLED
1 PT HEAVY CREAM, CHILLED
¼ CUP COLD WATER
¼ TSP SALT
1 TBSP HONEY (OPTIONAL)

SPECIAL EQUIPMENT:
1 SMALL GLASS MARBLE
1 QT CANNING JAR WITH A TIGHTLY FITTING LID

Makes 12 muffins and about 2 cups of strawberry butter

Make the muffins:

1 Preheat the oven to 350°F. In a large mixing bowl, combine the sugar, eggs, and vanilla. Fold in the zucchini and then the butter.

2 In a separate bowl, mix together the remaining muffin ingredients and gently stir them into the zucchini mixture, without overmixing.

3 Line a cupcake tin with cupcake liners. Use a spoon to distribute the muffin dough equally among the cups. The cups should be almost full. Bake on the middle rack of the oven until the muffins are golden brown and a toothpick or cake tester inserted into the middle comes out clean, about 25–30 minutes. Let cool on a baking rack for about 10 minutes.

While the muffins are baking, make the strawberry butter:

4 Cut the strawberries into tiny pieces and set aside. Pour the cream into the jar and drop in the marble. Close the jar tightly, and shake it continuously for about 5 minutes.

5 As the butter begins to thicken, keep shaking until a watery liquid (this is whey) separates from the fat and protein. Remove the cover from the jar and add the cold water. Seal the jar again and continue to shake for another 2–3 minutes. The butter should separate from the whey and water and solidify. Using a spoon, remove the marble from the jar. Scoop the butter out of the jar and while it's still soft, mix in the salt, honey (if using), and strawberries.

JOYCE'S GRANOLA

*From Joyce Quitasol, pastry chef
and co-owner of Joyce Bakeshop*

Despite the fact that Joyce Bakeshop is known for classic French pastries such as pillowy soft brioche and flaky croissants, their housemade granola is still a best seller. Made with both butter and maple syrup and a pile of nuts and seeds—this granola is rugged and chunky, as good on its own as with milk or cream—it's hardly health food either. Happily this recipe makes a generous amount that can be easily stored in an airtight container for up to 1 week. You can experiment with your favorite spices, nuts, and dried fruit, suggests Quitasol, but we think she's got an excellent mix fairly locked down.

1½ STICKS UNSALTED BUTTER
⅔ CUP HONEY
1 CUP MAPLE SYRUP
1 CUP LIGHT BROWN SUGAR
7 CUPS ROLLED OATS
1½ CUPS SLICED ALMONDS
1½ CUPS CHOPPED WALNUTS

1 CUP PUMPKIN SEEDS
1 CUP DRIED CRANBERRIES
1 CUP RAISINS
1 CUP CHOPPED DRIED APRICOTS

Makes about 3 quarts

1 Preheat the oven to 350°F. In a large saucepan, bring the butter, honey, maple syrup, and light brown sugar to a slow boil over medium-high heat. Stir in the rolled oats, nuts, and seeds until well coated with the butter mixture. Pour the granola directly onto a sheet pan and spread it out evenly.

2 Bake the mixture for about 15 minutes, until evenly brown, making sure to stir with a large spoon every 5 minutes to bake evenly and keep the mixture loose. Cool the granola until it reaches room temperature, and add the dried fruit. Store in an airtight container for up to 1 week.

BROOKLYN HOECAKES

From Millicent Souris,
Brooklyn baker and pastry chef

Where Millicent Souris bakes, *Edible Brooklyn* follows. We've eaten her incredible apple and berry pies, butter-drenched cinnamon buns, corn bread, and biscuits (likely the borough's best) at Diner, Marlowe & Sons, Queen's Hideaway, Egg, and most recently at Roebling Tea Room in Williamsburg, where her quince-tomato tarts and fat focaccia are always on our minds. (And don't get us started on her pickles, her gravy, or her oyster dressing.) This recipe, for rustic, pan-fried eighteenth-century cornmeal cakes made up and down the eastern seaboard, hails from *Maryland's Way*, an old recipe book from Souris's native Baltimore: "Neither thin like a pancake nor crumbly like a biscuit, these hoecakes are their own beast: crispy and firm on the outside," she says, "and creamy on the inside." Served either sweet or savory, they're delicious when paired with butter and molasses or maple syrup, or with collards—"They're for sopping," adds Souris. "I enjoy their versatility and the fact that people have to say 'hoecake' when they order them," she jokes: "Joy is in the little things, my friend." The key here, as with good corn bread, is to use the best-quality cornmeal you can find.

2 ¼ CUPS YELLOW OR WHITE
  CORNMEAL, COARSE
1 CUP ALL-PURPOSE FLOUR
3 TBSP WHITE SUGAR
1½ TBSP KOSHER SALT
1 TBSP BAKING POWDER
2½ STICKS COLD UNSALTED
  BUTTER, CUT INTO ¼-INCH TO
  ⅓-INCH CUBES

1 SCANT CUP BUTTERMILK
BUTTER OR LARD FOR FRYING

Serves 6–8

1 In a large bowl, mix together the cornmeal, flour, sugar, kosher salt, and baking powder. Scatter the butter over the dry ingredients. Quickly mix the butter into the dry ingredients with your fingers, using a sort of snapping motion between your thumb and middle finger until the mixture resembles crumbs.

2 Add the buttermilk and fold together loosely. The batter should ball up and be a little moist, but not really wet or sticky. If it is, dust some cornmeal or flour over it. Let the hoecake dough rest for 15 minutes.

3 Set a cast-iron skillet over a medium-high flame. Drop in a tablespoon or two of butter. It should melt upon contact, but not quickly burn. If it does, your pan is too hot and you should wipe it out and start again.

4 After the fat bubbles subside, place two 2-inch balls of batter in the pan. Let the balls sizzle in the pan for just a moment, and then flatten them using your index and middle fingers. Turn the heat down to medium. The hoecakes will crust up on one side and you should see them begin to darken on the bottom. After about 2 minutes, flip the cakes and press them down a bit with a spatula. When the bottom side becomes crisp and brown, they're done.

5 Remove the hoecakes from the pan to a paper towel to absorb some of the fat, and serve with any side or sauce you like, such as apple butter, crème fraîche, or roasted peppers.

BETSY'S RICOTTA AND FRUIT TARTINE

*From Betsy Devine, co-owner of
Salvatore Brooklyn Ricotta*

Betsy Devine and Rachel Mark, the owners of Salvatore Brooklyn Ricotta, did
not set out to make a dairy product so
dreamy—pillowy soft and ultracreamy—
that fans swear they eat the organic,
whole-milk ricotta straight from the tub
with a spoon. But after learning the ropes
on a trip to Italy, Devine started making
it in the kitchen of the restaurant where
she worked, and soon she and Mark were
making a living.

¼ CUP HIGH-QUALITY FRESH
  WHOLE-MILK RICOTTA
2 LARGE SLICES COUNTRY BREAD,
  TOASTED
4–6 THIN SLICES OF FRESH FRUIT
  (APPLES, PEACHES, PLUMS,
  OR STRAWBERRIES)

¼ CUP NUTTY GRANOLA
1 TBSP HONEY

Makes 2 tartines

1 Smear ricotta on each slice of toasted bread and cover with slices of
your favorite fruit.

2 Sprinkle granola on top, drizzle with honey, and serve immediately.

CAROLINE FIDANZA, CO-OWNER OF SALTIE

Where she cooks, Brooklyn follows.

There are plenty of those key moments in Brooklyn's restaurant rebirth—when al di lá started making ricotta malfatti in the late 1990s, say, or when The Grocery garnered its near-perfect Zagat Survey score in 2003—but one of the most crucial is the summer of 1998, when Caroline Fidanza was in between jobs.

Fidanza—now co-owner of the superb little sandwich and sweets shop called Saltie in Williamsburg—had just come back from a few weeks in France after a stint in the kitchen of the revered Manhattan restaurant Savoy. She'd heard that two business partners—Mark Firth and Andrew Tarlow—were looking for a chef for an old silver dining car they'd scored in the shadow of the Williamsburg Bridge on what was then a desolate corner. She quickly convinced the pair that instead of a short-order breakfast biz, Diner had to make "real food," and it needed to stay open for dinner.

Fidanza was right. While breakfast and lunch were lazy, dinner at Diner thrived, drawing visitors from across the East River not for the eternally hip aesthetic of tattoos and white tile, but for Fidanza's cooking, which is both simple and straightforward, but also seriously sexy. Steaks, roasted chicken,

and a killer burger, yes, but also a shaved corn salad, the milky sweet kernels tossed raw with chiles, scallions, and cherry tomatoes; spring radishes braised with butter, cream, and stock; and a wedge of the Spanish-olive-oil-soaked potato-egg cake called a tortilla still made by Fidanza each day at Saltie.

Fidanza's ingredient-forward focus is common these days, but she's both a master and a pioneer. It started with a mainly vegetarian culinary training at Manhattan's Natural Gourmet Institute and blossomed at Savoy, where famous founding chef Peter

Hoffman was still working in the kitchens. Today he's the textbook definition of a farm-to-table chef, but back in 1994, says Fidanza, "people didn't talk like that."

But Hoffman's focus—and insistence that every kitchen employee take turns visiting the farmers' market—made an impression nonetheless. "I knew," says Fidanza, "I was in the right place."

It was with that mind-set that she went on to help Firth and Tarlow create one of the borough's most cutting-edge restaurant groups, one that sourced from a roster of cool farmers and food makers before the mainstream even cared. After Diner came Marlowe & Sons, the gastropub and oyster bar next door, then Marlowe & Daughters, an ultra–specialty foods store and full-on butcher shop up the road. Despite her ways with radishes, in fact, Fidanza is one of those responsible for Brooklyn's current embrace of sustainably raised meats: with her lead, the restaurants removed all conventionally raised proteins from their menus, instead buying whole animals from farmers upstate. (Her colleague Tom Mylan, after learning the ropes at Marlowe, went on to open Meat Hook butcher shop nearby.)

These days there's very little meat on Fidanza's collaborative menu at Saltie: "We don't have the space." She shrugs, referring to the lack of room to break down a pig. Now Fidanza's fans come mainly for a coffee and a sticky bun, and for sandwiches such as the Captain's Daughter (pickled egg, salsa verde, and sardines on fat housemade focaccia) and the Little Chef (mortadella, pecorino, parsley, and olives), named after Fidanza herself.

POTATO TORTILLA

From Caroline Fidanza, chef and co-owner of Saltie café in Williamsburg

As the founding chef of Diner and Marlowe & Sons and a co-owner of the excellent sandwich shop called Saltie, Caroline Fidanza (see profile, opposite) has always made some of the very best food in Brooklyn. And this recipe has followed her everywhere she's cooked, beginning at the illustrious Manhattan restaurant Savoy, where she was required to make this classic Spanish tapas dish on a daily basis. "It's great to eat at any time of day," says Fidanza, who notes that the dish—essentially a beautiful, impressively large cake of eggs and thinly sliced potatoes—is also called potato Española or, in Spain, potato omelet. "It is luxurious and creamy and savory, made with all good ingredients." It's also grown beyond a staple of her menu to become a staple of life: "What used to be a daily chore has changed into a morning meditation," says Fidanza, "allowing me to repeat a task I know well as my first order of business, grounding and focusing me for the day." This recipe can be divided in half or even by thirds, says Fidanza. "Serve it as a main course with a salad, or in slivers as tapas or a starter course, and either warm or at room temperature, as the Spanish do. In my opinion it is also one of the most wonderful dishes one could possibly know how to prepare."

4 CUPS EXTRA-VIRGIN OLIVE OIL
12 MEDIUM YUKON GOLD POTATOES, PEELED AND SLICED INTO ⅛-INCH ROUNDS
2 MEDIUM YELLOW ONIONS, SLICED INTO ⅛-INCH ROUNDS

1 TBSP KOSHER SALT, PLUS EXTRA IF NEEDED
12 WHOLE EGGS

Serves 10–12 as tapas or a starter, 5–6 as a main course

1 Heat the olive oil in a large Dutch oven set over medium heat until shimmering. Add the potatoes, reduce the heat slightly, and sauté over medium-low heat until they are cooked about halfway through (enough to provide some resistance to the tip of a knife), about 8 minutes.

2 Add the onions and continue to cook until the potatoes are soft, another 5 minutes. Drain the mixture through a sieve or colander set over a bowl, and reserve the oil. Move the potato mixture to a large bowl and season well with kosher salt.

3 Let the potatoes and onions cool for about 10 minutes, but don't let them get cold. Break the eggs directly into the bowl of potatoes, and then vigorously but carefully fold the potatoes and eggs together with a wooden spoon until well incorporated, without breaking up the potatoes. Season again with salt.

4 Heat a 12-inch skillet. Add the reserved cooking oil so that it covers the bottom of the pan, and swirl it carefully so that it coats the sides. Heat the oil until it is smoking, and pour in the potato-egg mixture. Reduce the heat to low, and begin pulling the tortilla away from the sides of the pan with a rubber spatula, so that it doesn't stick. Shake the pan from side to side to make sure it isn't sticking, and let the egg set, running the spatula occasionally around the sides of the pan and rotating the pan on the burner, if needed.

5 In about 20 minutes, the sides of the tortilla should have stabilized. Place a large flat plate or pizza pan on top of the pan and invert the pan onto the plate. Using the spatula, gently slide the uncooked side of your tortilla back into the pan, running the spatula around the sides so that it doesn't stick, and continue to cook for about 5 minutes. Turn off the heat, let the tortilla sit for 5 minutes, and then flip it back out onto a large serving plate.

BACON-MAPLE-BOURBON COFFEE CARAMEL CORN

*From Jen King, pastry chef
and co-founder of Liddabit Sweets*

When Liz Gutman and Jen King—both graduates of The French Culinary Institute, where they met—joined forces to launch Liddabit Sweets, candy maker Frank Mars must have rolled over in his grave. In just two years the pair have earned wide praise for their confections, incorporating as many local and organic goods as they can into their small-batch bites, which include chewy beer and pretzel caramels made with ales from Brooklyn Brewery and pretzels from Martin's Pretzels. This particular snack, an adult version of the classic caramel corn you loved as a kid, is laced with bourbon, bacon, and coffee—a killer salty-sweet combo Jen discovered while experimenting with some of her boyfriend's favorite ingredients: "I was trying to figure out how to incorporate all three into a candy," she says. "I started to play around with this caramel corn, and I wasn't even planning on selling it, but before you knew it, people were asking for it."

1 STICK UNSALTED BUTTER	20 CUPS OF POPPED POPCORN
¼ CUP LIGHT CORN SYRUP	1½ TSP FINELY GROUND COFFEE
¼ CUP DARK (GRADE 8) MAPLE SYRUP	1 CUP COOKED BACON, CRUMBLED INTO PIECES
¼ CUP BOURBON	1 TSP BAKING SODA
2 CUPS SUGAR	
NONSTICK COOKING SPRAY	*Serves 8–10*

1 Melt the butter in a medium saucepan set over low heat. Stir in the light corn syrup, maple syrup, bourbon, and sugar. Increase the heat to medium-high, place a candy thermometer in the saucepan, and continue to cook until the temperature reads 300°F.

2 In the meantime, heavily coat a large bowl (or two, if necessary) with nonstick cooking spray, and add the popcorn. Also spray 2 spatulas and set aside.

3 When the bourbon mixture reaches 300°F, take it off the heat immediately and add the coffee, stirring well. Add the cooked bacon pieces and baking soda. Blend well until fully incorporated.

4 Carefully add the hot bourbon mixture to the popcorn and immediately toss with the spatulas until thoroughly coated. (Keep tossing the popcorn until it cools down a bit or the caramel corn will stick to itself. If that happens, spray on some more nonstick spray and it will separate.) Let cool completely before serving.

MAMA O'S PREMIUM KIMCHI SALSA

*From Kheedim Oh, owner of
Mama O's Premium Kimchi*

Like any good Korean boy, Kheedim Oh learned how to make kimchi from his mother, hence the name of his Brooklyn-based company. While Oh is now a master at using fermented vegetables in hyper-creative ways, this was the first "kimchi fusion dish," as he calls it, that he created. It's a salsa with a briny bite that premiered during Oh's first few months in business at a local foods fair held in Brooklyn every summer.

1 MEDIUM RED ONION, MINCED
3 MEDIUM RIPE TOMATOES, STEMMED AND CUT INTO ½-INCH DICE
1 SMALL BUNCH CILANTRO, MINCED
¼ CUP KIMCHI, CUT INTO ½-INCH DICE
JUICE FROM 3 LIMES
SALTED TORTILLA CHIPS, FOR SERVING

Serves 2

Mix together the onion, tomatoes, cilantro, and kimchi until well combined. Add the lime juice and mix again. Let rest a few minutes, and serve with salted tortilla chips.

ST. AGUR BLUE CHEESE DIP

From Zoe Singer, food writer

Zoe Singer is the food editor at *The Faster Times* and a prolific cookbook writer—she compiles *Food & Wine* magazine's yearly tome, for starters—as well as a contributor to *Edible Brooklyn*. She created this recipe for a story about the departure of the long-standing cheesemonger at the Park Slope Food Coop, a much-beloved local cooperative specialty foods market of which she is a member. Singer prefers using St. Agur here, "a French blue with a buttery mouth-feel, an elegant floral flavor, and an unusual freshness for a blue."

½ CUP WHOLE-MILK YOGURT
6 TBSP CREAMY BLUE CHEESE, PREFERABLY ST. AGUR
¼ CUP MAYONNAISE
2 TBSP MINCED FRESH CHIVES

Makes 1 generous cup

In a medium mixing bowl, mash the ingredients together with a fork, leaving some chunks of blue cheese. Serve at room temperature with, for example, sliced fennel bulb or blanched snap peas.

STAINED-GLASS POTATO CHIPS

From Annie Novak, founder of Growing Chefs and co-founder of Eagle Street Rooftop Farm

Annie Novak—a former educator at the New York Botanical Garden who was famously crowned one of the country's "hottest organic farmers" by the Huffington Post—set out in 2005 to reconnect city dwellers to the old-fashioned idea of "field to fork." Growing Chefs staffers aim to share their enthusiasm for nutritious, well-grown produce through good food—edible lessons made easier at Eagle Street Rooftop Farm, which Novak also helps run. The sky-high garden at the northern tip of Brooklyn features bees, chickens, a Sunday farm market, tidy rows, and a stunning view of Manhattan. It also stocks all the ingredients for this elegant salty little snack—which looks a bit like stained glass and tastes a lot like an herby potato chip.

2 TBSP UNSALTED BUTTER, MELTED
3 LARGE, WAXY POTATOES, CUT LENGTHWISE INTO ¹⁄₁₆-INCH SLICES USING A MANDOLIN OR HANDHELD SLICER
½ CUP FLAT PARSLEY LEAVES, WASHED AND DRIED
½ CUP BASIL LEAVES, WASHED AND DRIED
2 LONG SPRIGS FRESH ROSEMARY
SALT

Serves 6

1 Preheat the oven to 375°F.

2 Lightly butter half of the potato slices on one side using a pastry brush and place them buttered side down on sheet pans lined with parchment.

3 Top each slice with 1 leaf of parsley, 1 leaf of basil, and about 3 rosemary leaves in the center. Sandwich with another potato slice, lightly buttering the outside. Press gently on each potato package to bind and sprinkle tops with salt to taste.

4 Bake for about 15 minutes, flipping them over every 5 minutes to be sure they're not burning. Serve immediately, sprinkled with more salt, if you like.

LIFT (PICKLED TURNIPS) WITH *LEBANY* AND *ZAATAR*

From Christine Whelan, owner of Sahadi's Market

Since 1948, the family-owned Sahadi's has remained one of Brooklyn's must-visit destinations for delicacies, not just for its top-tier Middle Eastern foods—hummus, kibbi, grape leaves—but for its chaotic traditions. You take a number and you wait (and wait) your turn for a clerk and for bags of hard-to-find fresh almonds, excellent spices, or tubs of the pink pickled turnips Middle Easterners call *lift*, often seen tucked into falafel or other sandwiches. Made across the Middle East, *lift* is served at room temperature as part of a mix of pickles, dips, and snacks known as *meze*. In her Lebanese family, says Christine Whelan, it's always eaten with a dollop of thick, strained yogurt called *lebany*, which is sprinkled with *zaatar*, a bright green spice mix made from sesame seeds, sumac, and other spices, depending on your country of origin and your family recipe. Speaking of recipes, these have been in Whelan's family for decades, if not centuries, considering the first of the Sahadis came to New York City in 1898.

FOR THE *LIFT*:

2 LB SMALL TURNIPS, UNPEELED, SCRUBBED, AND QUARTERED

2 SMALL BEETS (GREENS REMOVED), UNPEELED, SCRUBBED, AND QUARTERED

¾ CUP KOSHER SALT

8 CUPS WATER

4 CUPS DISTILLED WHITE VINEGAR

FOR THE *LEBANY* WITH *ZAATAR*:

1 LB *LEBANY*, OR MIDDLE EASTERN DRAINED YOGURT

2 TBSP PLUS 2 TSP *ZAATAR* SPICE

1 CLOVE GARLIC, MINCED

2 TBSP EXTRA-VIRGIN OLIVE OIL

Makes about 12 pita breads filled with lift *and* lebany, *depending on how full you make them.*

Make the *lift*:

1 Place the turnips and beets together in a nonreactive bowl, preferably glass or ceramic. In a large bowl, combine the salt, water, and vinegar, and blend until the salt has dissolved and the brine is clear.

2 Pour the brine over the turnip and beet mixture; it should be completely submerged (weight the mixture down with a small plate to keep all the vegetables in the brine). Discard any remaining brine. Leave at room temperature 4 hours and then refrigerate for 48 hours, or until pickled to your taste. Use within 2 weeks.

Once the pickles are to your liking, make the *lebany*:

3 Blend the *lebany* with the 2 tablespoons *zaatar* and garlic in a small bowl until well mixed. Spread the mixture out on a platter and drizzle with olive oil. Sprinkle with the remaining 2 teaspoons *zaatar* or serve in a bowl with a drizzle of olive oil and a sprinkle of *zaatar* on top. Serve in pita bread.

FLYING PIGS FARM'S *CHICHARONNES*

*From Mike Yezzi and Jen Small,
owners of Flying Pigs Farm*

Mike Yezzi and his wife, Jen Small, are now some of New York City's top pork purveyors, but well before they'd even given up their jobs in social work to farm full-time, the very first place they ever sold their meat was at Brooklyn's downtown farmers' market. They still come into the borough each Saturday, selling out of bacon by 11 a.m. Needless to say, they use every part of the pig at home, and this recipe is one that their six-year-old daughter, Jane, finds especially addictive. Ask your butcher or a pork producer at your local farmers' market if they can help you find pork back fat with the skin still on.

Note: this recipe takes 2–3 days.

1 8-INCH BY 6-INCH PIECE OF PORK
BACK FAT, SKIN ON

SALT

Makes about 10 dozen chicharonnes

1 Fill a large stock pot with water, add the back fat, and gently simmer over medium heat for 1 hour, or until the skin is tender. (You should be able to easily poke through it with a butter knife.) Remove and, when cool enough to handle, gently scrape all the fat away from the skin with a spoon, removing as much fat as possible.

2 Put the scraped fat in a saucepan and gently cook over low heat so that it breaks down. Strain and reserve the liquid fat in the refrigerator.

3 Slice the skin into 1-inch by ⅓-inch strips and place on sheet of parchment paper or drying rack. Allow the strips to dry out, uncovered, at room temperature for 2–3 days. They should snap cleanly in half when dry.

4 Heat the reserved fat in a deep, heavyweight skillet over medium-high heat until it is almost smoking. Working quickly in batches, add the strips of dried skin to the fat. They should puff and twist immediately (if they do not, the oil is not hot enough or the skin is not dry enough). Turn the skin gently in the fat until it stops increasing in size and the bubbles around it subside. Cook to golden brown (or deep brown if you like a more robust flavor) and season with salt to taste. The *chicharonnes* will last a few days in a sealed container at room temperature.

SPICY OLIVE HUMMUS

From Michael Hearst, musician

A multitalented composer and musician, Michael Hearst has worked with bands such as The Magnetic Fields and the Kronos Quartet and performed at Carnegie Hall. But we're most fond of his work titled "Songs for Ice Cream Trucks," featuring his take on the jingles that ring out from the trucks that cruise Brooklyn streets each summer. While this addictively creamy and uniquely spiced hummus—thanks to Hearst's multiculti addition of olives, cumin, and garlicky Asian hot sauce—isn't as decadent as a cone of chocolate soft serve, it's probably a smarter hunger killer to have on hand. "My Park Slope apartment doubles as my recording studio," says Hearst. "Quite often guest musicians come over to add tracks to songs I'm working on. Because it's my apartment, I always feel the need to offer snacks."

Edible Tip

The very thing that makes olives so addictive is the brine that they come packed in, so don't let it go to waste! Use it in place of salt, as in this recipe. The result is a sharper hit of flavor.

1 TBSP EXTRA-VIRGIN OLIVE OIL
1 SMALL CLOVE GARLIC
1 (16 OZ) CAN CHICKPEAS, DRAINED AND RINSED
2 TBSP TAHINI
⅓ CUP WATER
¼ CUP BOTTLED PITTED GREEN OLIVES (ABOUT 8–10), BRINE RESERVED
½ TSP CHILI-GARLIC SAUCE OR SRIRACHA HOT SAUCE
¼ TSP GROUND CUMIN
¼ TSP FRESHLY GROUND BLACK PEPPER
½ TSP CHOPPED FRESH PARSLEY

Makes about 2 cups

1 Place the olive oil and garlic in the bowl of a food processor and pulse on and off for 30 seconds. Add the chickpeas, tahini, and water. Turn food processor on and leave on, adding the olives, olive brine, chili-garlic sauce, cumin, pepper, and parsley. Continue blending for another 2 minutes.

2 Transfer to a bowl and serve with crackers or carrots and celery. This dip is also great in a sandwich.

SCRATCHBREAD FOCACCIA

*From Matthew J. Tilden,
founder of SCRATCHbread*

Matthew Tilden makes luscious rustic rosemary–sea salt scones and breads—each craggy, densely delicious loaf tied with twine, and almost all of them made with about 80 percent organic flours. He got his start using the brick ovens at Toby's Public House, an upscale pizzeria, when they weren't in use, and also sells at the Brooklyn Flea (see profile, page 74). Happily, he has recently opened his very own operation in the neighborhood of Bed-Stuy. This recipe, for one of his most coveted creations, will yield wonderful results if you follow Tilden's method for massaging as much olive oil as you can into the dough. The trick, he says, is using your fingers to "play" the dough as if it's a piano.

Edible Tip

Like many commercial bakers, Tilden uses fresh, or "compressed" or "brick" yeast, which works faster and is stronger than active dry yeast but must be kept refrigerated and usually comes in 0.6-ounce or 2-ounce foil-wrapped cakes. It's found at many supermarkets, but you can substitute 1 package active dry yeast per ounce of fresh yeast.

1 OZ COMPRESSED, OR "BRICK," YEAST
1 TBSP HONEY
6 TBSP (1 OZ) COARSE GRAY SEA SALT, PLUS MORE FOR SPRINKLING
4½ CUPS (2 LB) ALL-PURPOSE UNBLEACHED UNBROMATED FLOUR, PREFERABLY ORGANIC
1¾ CUPS PLUS 2 TBSP 00 DURUM WHEAT FLOUR
2 TBSP EXTRA-VIRGIN OLIVE OIL, PLUS MORE FOR COATING THE FOCACCIA
¼ CUP FRESH ROSEMARY LEAVES

Makes 1 large sheet-pan-size loaf

1 Mix yeast, honey, and salt with 2¾ cups plus 2 tablespoons warm water (between 90 and 100°F) and let dissolve. Set aside.

2 In the bowl of a stand mixer with the dough hook attached, add both flours and the yeast mixture and incorporate into a sticky, strandy dough, or what Tilden refers to as a "shaggy mass." Continue mixing until the dough comes together and begins pulling away from the sides of the bowl, about 1½ minutes. Add 2 tablespoons olive oil and mix in for about 20 seconds.

3 Cover bowl loosely with a tea towel and let the dough rise until doubled, about an hour and a half. Once the dough is doubled in size and very fluffy, punch it down, cover it, and let it rest for about another 35–45 minutes.

4 Once the dough has become fluffy again, turn it out onto a clean, dry surface, fold it into a tight mass, and knead it well. "Punch it, elbow it, release all frustrations," says Tilden, "as you are basically giving it life by pulverizing it. So consider this a good deed to the dough." Let the well-kneaded dough rest for about 15 minutes, cover it with olive oil and gently pat into a heavy nonstick sheet pan.

5 Preheat the oven to 375°F. Be sure the dough is coated with oil, massaging it in with your fingertips, adding more oil as you do so, and using your fingers to form crevasses for the olive oil to collect in.

6 After 15 minutes, the dough should have risen again slightly and become fluffy. Sprinkle on the rosemary and more sea salt. Bake for about 35 minutes, rotating the pan halfway through, until the bread is a dark golden brown. Immediately and carefully remove the hot bread from the oven and place on a cooling rack to let the crust form. Let cool to room temperature and cut into squares.

HONEYED NUTS AND BLUE CHEESE

From Grai St. Clair Rice,
co-founder of HoneybeeLives

Grai St. Clair Rice teaches Brooklynites how to raise bees on rooftops and in backyards—it became legal in 2010—and as a result she's got access to plenty of top-grade honey, which she likes to jar with nuts and red chile flakes and give to friends with a wedge of good blue cheese. "This recipe is a wonderful holiday treat for beekeepers and beekeepers' friends," she says. "It is surely not inexpensive, with the nuts and the honey," she adds. "However, the savory-sweet experience is worth it. It offers a glorious contrast to the salty, earthy taste of the blue cheese."

2 TBSP PINE NUTS
¼ CUP WALNUT HALVES
¼ CUP PECAN HALVES
¼ HAZELNUTS
½ CUP RAW HONEY

1 TSP CRUSHED RED PEPPER
   FLAKES (OPTIONAL)
½ LB WEDGE BLUE CHEESE

Serves 6

1 Preheat the oven to 350°F.

2 Lay the nuts on baking sheets in a single layer, separating the pine nuts, which cook more quickly, and the hazelnuts, whose papery outer skin will flake off after roasting.

3 Roast the pine nuts until they are well toasted, about 3 minutes, and remove them from the oven. Roast the rest of the nuts for 7–10 minutes more, shaking the baking sheets gently a couple of times during roasting. Remove the pans from the oven, and let the nuts cool.

4 Once the nuts have cooled, clean the hazelnuts of their skins by rubbing them with a clean tea towel and mix all the nuts together with the honey, adding the red pepper flakes, if using.

5 Serve in a bowl alongside a wedge of blue cheese, or pour into clean jars to give as gifts.

CHOCOLATE-COVERED KALE CHIPS

*From Daniel Sklaar, founder of
Fine & Raw Chocolate*

You'd likely never guess that Fine & Raw's Brooklyn-made line of chocolates (sometimes sold wrapped in old seventies pinup posters) are created using very low heat during the cooking process, unlike other bars. This helps to retain the bean's layers of flavors and antioxidants, says owner Daniel Sklaar, a raw chef and former financial analyst who carefully sources his cacao from small farms. This recipe is just as surprising. Over the past few years, baked kale chips (sometimes called "crack kale" for their addictive properties) have made their way into plenty of kitchens. The idea was first floated by French chef Jacques Pepin, but this is the first variation we've seen that's candy coated. Sklaar uses his own sea salt dark chocolate bar in this recipe, but you could substitute another dark chocolate bar flavored with sea salt.

1 BUNCH SMALL- TO MEDIUM-LEAF KALE, WASHED, DRIED, AND STEMMED
1 TBSP TAMARI SAUCE
1 TBSP EXTRA-VIRGIN OLIVE OIL
½ TSP SEA SALT
¼ TSP FRESHLY GROUND BLACK PEPPER
4 OZ SEA SALT–FLAVORED DARK CHOCOLATE, SUCH AS FINE & RAW

Makes about 1 dozen chips

1 Preheat the oven to 350°F.

2 Place the kale in a large bowl, drizzle in the tamari and oil, and sprinkle with sea salt and pepper. Mix and massage the kale with your hands until all the ingredients have coated the leaves.

3 Bake the kale on a sheet pan until it begins to dry out and becomes crispy and the ends begin to brown, about 10–15 minutes. Transfer to a rack to cool completely.

4 Meanwhile, melt the chocolate slowly in a double boiler set over low heat. Dip each piece of kale into the chocolate so that three-quarters of the leaf is coated. Place the kale on a plate or wax-paper-covered tray in the refrigerator to allow the chocolate to harden. Can be stored overnight in an airtight container and served the next day if necessary.

WHITE BEAN PUREE

*From Justin Philips,
co-owner of Beer Table*

Ordering an ale at Beer Table is akin to ordering a glass of white at a wine bar: that's just the beginning. Your bartender—make that your beer sommelier—will gladly walk you through this elegant little tasting room's incredibly large menu of the world's best craft beers, explaining the various aromas, what you'll sense on the nose and in the mouth, the colors and flavors you now find through the menu at your fingertips. In addition to their quaffs, Justin and Tricia, the couple behind Beer Table, offer some killer appetizers meant to be shared among beer drinkers at Beer Table's communal countertops.

1 HEAD GARLIC, WHOLE
2 TBSP EXTRA-VIRGIN OLIVE OIL
½ TBSP KOSHER SALT
FRESHLY GROUND BLACK PEPPER
16 OZ CANNED CANNELLINI BEANS, DRAINED
JUICE FROM 1 SMALL LEMON
½ CUP PLAIN YOGURT

1 SMALL HOT FRESH RED CHILE PEPPER, THINLY SLICED ON THE BIAS
SEA SALT
TOAST FOR SERVING

Serves 4

1 Preheat the oven to 425°F. Cut off the top of the head of garlic. Lay the garlic on a sheet of aluminum foil, drizzle with 1 tablespoon of the olive oil, sprinkle with the kosher salt and pepper, and wrap with the foil. Roast for 45 minutes, until tender, and let cool.

2 Squeeze the meat from the roasted cloves into a food processor. Add the beans, lemon juice, and yogurt and puree until creamy and smooth. Add kosher salt to taste and serve on toast topped with the fresh red chile, a drizzle of olive oil, and a pinch of sea salt.

ROASTED CAULIFLOWER SALAD

1 CUP CAULIFLOWER FLORETS,
SLICED OR BROKEN INTO
BITE-SIZE PIECES
1 TBSP LEMON JUICE
1 TBSP EXTRA-VIRGIN OLIVE OIL
4–6 LARGE LEAVES OF FRESH
PARSLEY, FOR GARNISH

4 RINGS OF PICKLED RED ONIONS,
CUT IN HALF
1 TBSP CAPERS
1 TSP CRUSHED RED PEPPER
FLAKES
PINCH OF COARSE GRAY SEA SALT

Serves 4

1 Preheat the oven to 450°F. Place the cauliflower in a baking dish and roast until it blackens slightly on the edges, 7–10 minutes.

2 Toss the cauliflower right as it comes out of the oven with a few drops of lemon juice and olive oil to taste. Use the remaining lemon juice and olive oil to dress the parsley leaves. Top with cauliflower and sprinkle with the remaining ingredients.

CHAPTER 2

FINGER FOOD, PICKLES, AND SIDES

Like most great American food cities, Brooklyn is in the throes of a serious produce obsession. Here a few slender vinaigrette-dressed haricot verts are serious dining; one restaurant's cauliflower "two ways" is a neighborhood obsession; fresh-cut kale salads are de rigueur; and humble sweet potato–scallion pancakes or green-chile-spiked black-eyed peas are delights. Home picklers, meanwhile, tote home cases of cucumbers, radishes, and ramps from the borough's fantastic farmers' markets. Their handiwork is destined not just for jars, but for sandwiches, smorgasbords, and even soups, like pickler Rick Field's Polish potato and sausage potage—a modern Brooklyn-based creation if there ever was one.

SAUSAGE AND CUCUMBER GRINDERS
WITH HOT PEPPER JELLY

From Cathy Erway, author of
NotEatingOutinNY.com

In the summer of 2010, author, food blogger, cook, and gardener Cathy Erway—she's one of the bigger boosters of the city's local and sustainable foods scene—helped Brooklyn's Sixpoint Brewery put in a rooftop farm and then started making the brewers lunch from the harvests (complete with eggs from chickens fed a rich diet of spent grain). "This was a really easy, make-your-own-sandwich lunch that I served at the brewhouse," she says of her "tummy-filling and crowd-pleasing" creation, which borrows its yin and yang of warm, fatty sausages and crispy, cooling vegetables from the Vietnamese sandwich called a *banh mi*. While her beer brats and hot pepper jelly are from nearby farmers, the cukes, baby lettuces, and shallots are all roof-raised in Brooklyn—and her coarse-grain mustard was even made with Sixpoint brews.

FOR THE PICKLED SHALLOTS:
1 TSP SUGAR
1 TSP SALT
½ CUP RED WINE VINEGAR
2 TBSP WARM WATER
1 SHALLOT, THINLY SLICED

FOR THE SANDWICHES:
3 FRESH BRATWURSTS
3–4 SMALL CUCUMBERS,
   SUCH AS PERSIAN OR KIRBY
6 HOAGIE ROLLS, SPLIT
BABY LETTUCES, FOR TOPPING
HOT PEPPER JELLY, FOR SERVING
COARSE-GRAIN MUSTARD,
   FOR SERVING (OPTIONAL)

Makes 6 sandwiches

Make the pickled shallots:

1 In a large Mason jar, stir together the sugar and salt with the vinegar and water until dissolved. Add the shallot slices, cover, and chill to quick-pickle while you prepare the rest of the ingredients. (Pickled shallots will last up to one week refrigerated.)

To make the sandwiches:

2 Place a heavy-bottomed, preferably cast-iron pan over medium heat and brown the bratwursts, turning occasionally, until fully cooked and firm, about 5 minutes (depending on the width of the sausages). Remove from pan and let cool a few minutes. Slice on the bias into 1- or 1½-inch pieces.

3 Trim the stems from the cucumbers and cut on the bias into 1 or 1½-inch pieces. Assemble the grinders by placing alternating pieces of sausage and cucumber on the hoagie rolls and top with the pickled shallots, lettuces, hot pepper jelly, and mustard.

FRESH MASA AND HANDMADE TORTILLAS

From Jacques Gautier, chef/owner of Palo Santo restaurant in Park Slope

Chef Jacques Gautier learned plenty for his Pan-Latin restaurant from his Haitian, Cuban, Dominican, and Puerto Rican relatives, but he also gets lessons from his kitchen crew, who are primarily Mexican immigrants. It was their influence that led to one of Palo Santo's best sellers: steaming hot homemade tortillas, fragrant with the scent of toasted corn. Unlike most tortillas sold, even in Mexico, the masa, or dough, for these is made with freshly ground kernels from what's sold as Indian corn, instead of prepared flour, and as a result they're practically a meal themselves. "Once you have made the tortillas, the hard work is done and you can easily turn them into tacos by filling them with cooked meat, fish, or veggies and topping them with avocado, hot sauce, and cilantro," says Gautier. Or use the dough to make tamales or empanadas.

Edible Tip

"Ever wonder if what's sold in the fall as 'Indian corn' is edible?" asks Jacques Gautier. "You hang it up as a decoration, and then what? Well, it might be a little bit hard to work with but it makes delicious tortillas." The only other ingredient you'll need is mineral lime, or *cal*, which is found at most Latin or Mexican supermarkets.

1 LB DRIED INDIAN CORN, OR OTHER DRIED CORN IF INDIAN CORN IS HARD TO FIND (FROM ABOUT 6 COBS)

2 TSP MINERAL LIME (*CAL* IN SPANISH)

1 TBSP SALT

OIL OR LARD FOR COOKING THE TORTILLAS

Makes about 3 dozen tortillas

1 Break the corn off the cob by holding it firmly with both hands and twisting to loosen the kernels. Then break the cob in the middle and work the kernels off with your thumbs.

2 Put the kernels into a large pot with the lime and cover with water. Simmer over low heat for an hour or so, until the kernels are soft but not mushy. Let them cool in the liquid to room temperature.

3 Strain out the boiled corn (reserving the liquid) and grind it using a meat grinder, food processor, high-powered blender, or grain mill on a coarse setting. Then process the corn a second time (on a finer setting, if using a grinder or mill) with a tablespoon or two of the cooking liquid—just enough so the mixture forms a pastelike dough. Add the salt and work the masa with your hands to make it smoother. Add a little bit more of the cooking liquid if necessary. The finished masa should be smooth, moist, and workable, but not sticky or loose.

4 Form the masa into 1-inch balls. Heat a griddle, preferably cast-iron, over a medium flame and grease lightly with a little oil. Line a tortilla press with plastic wrap or wax paper and press the balls, a few at a time (however many will fit onto your griddle), into tortillas about 4 inches across. (If you don't have a tortilla press, flatten the balls between plastic grocery bags using a heavy book.)

5 Turn the tortillas over onto the hot griddle. Flip them once they are firm enough and slightly toasted, and cook on the other side. Keep warm under a towel or in a plastic tortilla steamer until all are cooked. Use for making tacos or to serve alongside a Mexican meal, such as the salsa verde and eggs on page 5.

THE TORTILLA TRIANGLE

In Brooklyn's masa mecca, Mexican bakeries are creating a new indigenous industry.

Stepping out of the subway at the Jefferson stop on the L train is an exercise in olfactory entrancement. Follow the flight of stairs up to Starr Street and you land nearly at the entrance of Tortilleria Mexicana Los Hermanos. The warm minerality of cooked corn stretches over the block, and you can almost float on the curls of aroma into the factory, dreaming of the brown-specked tortillas that await you.

This area, where the neighborhoods of Bushwick and East Williamsburg overlap, is redolent of its industrial past and present, with steel-manufacturing plants, trucking depots, and low-slung warehouses lining Flushing Avenue. By the 1990s, a new industry joined them: tortilla production, bringing with it the centuries-old scent of toasted maize. The neighborhood was soon dubbed the "Tortilla Triangle" for its three Mexican-owned tortilla factories, or tortillerias: Buena Vista, Plaza Piaxtla, and Chinantla. With the addition of Los Hermanos and Tenochtitlan 2000, the triangle has been transformed into a corn-centered square, of sorts—maybe you'd even call it kernel shaped.

Whatever you name it, the area now cranks out millions of tortillas daily, representing the purchasing power of the growing local Latino community (sixty-nine thousand Mexicans have moved to New York City since 2000, according to the 2008 census) and the growing national taste for the flat corn disks. These tortillerias offer soft corn stacks at retail, but their primary business is bodegas, supermarkets, and upscale Manhattan restaurants. They even send their delivery vans to shops in New Jersey.

For authentic tortillas, freshness and accessibility are key; competition is fierce and brand loyalties ride high. All of the tortillerias get their corn-flour base, called masa, from a Maseca milling plant in Indiana—the days when most tortillerias made their own have passed, even in Mexico. But base material is where the similarities end. Production style and masa-to-water ratio create different textures and flavors among the brands, distinguishing tastes for the city's increasing numbers of tortilla connoisseurs. (Buena Vista's disks vary in thickness from stack to stack, while the tortillas of Los Hermanos have a pleasant ruddy feel.)

Many of the tortillerias, in fact, have expanded their companies to include sister businesses. Marcelina's Mexican Foods, a storefront on Flushing Avenue, is an offshoot of Plaza Piaxtla.

They import Mexican sodas and chiles but make their own Mexican-style *queso fresco*, *crema*, and *hebra* cheese. Hermanos took on new ground when they started hawking tacos and tortas. Owner Maurcelino Lazaro remembers when they "sat a little *carito* outside the warehouse when the weather was nice." They eventually dragged the cart inside as a makeshift taqueria. When the craving for a bean-slathered *al pastor* torta struck, you would enter the warehouse and sit down at a rickety communal table, passing limes and hot sauce to hair-netted workers on their lunch break. The rhythmic metallic tings of huge masa mixers and conveyer belts peppered the sound track while women bagged and boxed stacks of fresh tortillas.

When the NYC Department of Health ordered Lazaro to stop the informality, he closed the factory for two months to make renovations. There is now a restaurant within the tortilleria: it's almost a living diorama of a late-seventies Mexican diner, with particleboard ceilings, a long counter, and mosaic tile. You can still peer in at the tortilla making, and the carne enchilada, or spicy pork, is just as good.

The tortillas, of course, are outstanding.

SOUTHERN CALIFORNIA-STYLE BURRITO BEANS

From Tom Mylan,
butcher and co-owner of
The Meat Hook in Williamsburg

One of the country's most famous masters of meat and most widely recognized Brooklyn food entrepreneurs, Tom Mylan now helps run The Meat Hook, an artisanal butcher shop inside the Brooklyn Kitchen (see profile, page 42). So it's no surprise that the key ingredient in these killer refried beans is lard. "I went to high school in Orange County, California," says Mylan, "where the answer, seven times out of ten, to the question 'Hey, what do you want to eat?' is the simple pleasure of a bean and cheese burrito with extra cheese and extra green sauce."

Edible Tip

Tom Mylan uses his own Meat Hook–made lard to make better beans, and for maximum deliciousness you should follow his lead and use lard rendered from good-quality pork rather than commercially sold brands, which are highly processed and much less flavorful. Check your local farmers' market for the real thing.

1 LARGE ONION, ROUGHLY CHOPPED (ABOUT 1 CUP)

2 CUPS LARD

1 (16 OZ) PACKAGE OF DRIED PINTO BEANS, PREFERABLY GOYA, SOAKED IN WATER OVERNIGHT AND DRAINED

2 BAY LEAVES

SALT

Serves 8–10

1 In a large pot over medium-high heat, sweat the onion in 2 tablespoons of lard. Add the beans, bay leaves, remaining lard, and, if the beans are still a bit dry and not yet tender, 1 cup of water.

2 Allow the pot to simmer at low heat for an hour or more, until the beans are soft, adding water if needed. Remove the bay leaves, add salt to taste, and blend with an immersion blender or potato masher. Add more lard to taste, if you like.

3 Serve in a tortilla with some shredded cheese.

GRILLED CHEESE AND SPICY PICKLE SANDWICH

From Anne Saxelby,
founder of Saxelby Cheesemongers

Anne Saxelby is practically the New York City spokeswoman for the artisanal American cheese movement. Her specialty cheese shop, despite its tiny size, is one of the best in the country, we'd wager, for its incredible selection of American cheeses and for Saxelby's knowledge of flavor, cheese making, and sustainable dairy farming, which she delivers not just behind the counter, but on the field trips she leads to local farms and on her Internet radio show hosted by Brooklyn's own Heritage Radio Network. She also makes some of the best damn grilled cheese sandwiches you'll ever eat, thanks to their secret weapon—Brooklyn-made pickles. "Ever since Rick Field of Rick's Picks asked us to collaborate with him for NYC's Pickle Day," says Saxelby, "I've been hooked on grilled cheese and pickle sandwiches."

1 SANDWICH-SIZE PIECE THICK FOCACCIA

2 OZ LANDAFF, THINLY SLICED AND RINDS LEFT ON, OR USE ANY CAERPHILLY-STYLE CHEESE

6 RICK'S PICKS HOTTIES PICKLE CHIPS, SLICED LENGTHWISE, OR USE ANY SPICY PICKLE CHIPS

Makes 1 sandwich

1 Preheat a panini or sandwich press or heat a nonstick or cast-iron skillet over medium heat.

2 Slice the focaccia lengthwise. Layer the bottom half first with the cheese, then with the pickles. Replace the top half of the bread.

3 Toast your sandwich in the press until golden brown, or heat it in the pan, preferably held down with another pan or bacon press, flipping it once when the bottom has browned.

Edible Tip

Landaff and Rick's Picks Sriracha-spiced Hotties work particularly well together. Landaff is a buttery, mild cow's milk cheese, similar to Welsh Caerphilly, made in small batches in New Hampshire. It's available in some specialty cheese shops or at *LandaffCreamery.com*, and you can find Rick's Picks at Whole Foods nationwide.

BREAD-AND-BUTTER PICKLES

*From Chris Forbes and Evelyn Evers,
founders of Sour Puss Pickles*

Brooklyn is a city of great modern picklers, such as Chris Forbes and Evelyn Evers of Sour Puss. They take "the classic southern 'grandmother' pickle," as they call the bread-and-butters their own Oklahoma and Florida grandmas made, and mellow out their overly sweet edge with aromatics such as dried ginger, juniper berries, and celery seed. Ever the Southern expatriates, Forbes and Evers recommend you pair them with fried chicken or add them to a Cubano-like sandwich "with salty pork, piquant mustard, and a sharp cheese—preferably pressed or toasted."

5 LB KIRBY CUCUMBERS
3⅓ CUPS HIGH-ACID APPLE CIDER
 VINEGAR (AT LEAST 7% ACIDITY)
1⅛ CUPS ORGANIC CANE SUGAR
⅛ CUP KOSHER SALT
3 TSP BLACK PEPPERCORNS
3 TSP GROUND GINGER
2 TSP CELERY SEED

2 TSP GROUND ALLSPICE
2 TSP JUNIPER BERRIES
2 TBSP YELLOW MUSTARD SEEDS

SPECIAL EQUIPMENT:
6 CANNING JARS (1 PT) WITH LIDS

Makes 6 pints of pickles

1 Place the cucumbers in a large stock pot filled with cold water, weighing them down with a plate to ensure all are submerged, while the jars and lids are being sterilized. Meanwhile, bring another large pot of water to a low rolling boil and sterilize the jars and lids by boiling them for 20 minutes.

2 Put 5 cups water and the apple cider vinegar, sugar, and salt into a large pot and bring to a simmer over medium-high heat. Remove the cucumbers from their pot and slice into discs with a knife (or use a crinkle cutter, easily found at restaurant supply shops). Set aside.

3 In a skillet, lightly toast the black peppercorns, ginger, celery seed, allspice, and juniper berries. Add to the apple cider brine and bring to a low boil. Add the sliced cucumbers and return to a boil.

4 When all the cucumbers have changed in color from grass green to brownish mustard green (usually about 10 minutes) turn off the heat and let sit for 15 minutes. Distribute the cucumbers and spices, including the mustard seeds, between the jars and top with the brine, making sure the jars are full to just below the rim. Wipe the rims with a hot towel to clean off the excess sugar and brine. Place a clean, sterilized lid on each jar and close, but don't tighten all the way.

5 Return the pot of water to a boil. To seal the jars, immerse them in boiling water for 10 minutes. Remove with rubber tongs and let sit for 8–10 hours. Do not disturb the jars. The lids should seal as they cool. If the lids are suctioned downward and there is no flexibility, they are sealed and can be stored in the pantry for up to 14 months. If not, the jars can be kept in the refrigerator for up to 2 weeks.

PEOPLE'S PICKLE POLISH POTATO POTAGE
WITH BRINED CROUTONS

*From Rick Field,
founder and co-owner of Rick's Picks*

One of Brooklyn's first and most successful farm-friendly picklers—his products are now in Whole Foods nationwide—Rick Field admits to two passions beyond pickles. The first is alliteration, hence the catchy name of this hearty dish, and the second is soup, which he makes every weekend, brown bagging the leftovers to work. Many of his favorites are ultracheap concoctions made with pickles, naturally, and also potatoes: He recommends creamy German butterballs for this dish (especially those from farmer Bill Maxwell, who works the same Saturday farmers' market outside Park Slope's Prospect Park as Field). "Quality potatoes, when they are cooked down and blended in a food processor or with an immersion blender, will lend a natural creaminess to a puree or 'cream of' soup that usually eliminates the need for fatty cream itself while adding more flavor," says Field. This particular creation proves his point. The brined croutons in this recipe are another tasty surprise and not something you find often in recipes. You'll want to use them on salads and in other dishes too.

1½ STICKS UNSALTED BUTTER
4 TBSP BRINE FROM A JAR OF PICKLED RED PEPPERS (SUCH AS RICK'S PICKS' PEPI PEP PEPS, WHICH ARE ROASTED RED PEPPERS THAT ARE PICKLED IN THEIR JUICE WITH GINGER AND GARLIC)
1 BAGUETTE, SLICED INTO ½-INCH ROUNDS
2 LARGE YELLOW ONIONS, ROUGHLY CHOPPED
3 LB POTATOES (PREFERABLY GERMAN BUTTERBALL, YUKON GOLD, OR RED BLISS), CUT INTO 1-INCH CUBES

2 QT LOW-SODIUM CHICKEN STOCK
JUICE FROM 1 LEMON
FRESHLY GROUND BLACK PEPPER
2 CUPS MILK, PLUS EXTRA FOR THINNING THE SOUP
1 JAR DILL PICKLE CHIPS (SUCH AS RICK'S PICKS THE PEOPLE'S PICKLE), DRAINED AND CHOPPED INTO ½-INCH CUBES; 3 TBSP STRAINED BRINE RESERVED
1 SMALL BUNCH DILL, MINCED
1 SMALL BUNCH CHIVES, MINCED

Serves 10

1 To make the croutons: preheat the oven to 450°F. Melt half a stick of butter in a sauté pan over low heat. Add the brine from the pickled red peppers, making sure to include a few bits of spices from the jar if there are any, and whisk together till smooth. Brush each of the rounds of bread with the butter-brine mixture on both sides, place on a nonstick baking sheet, and bake for about 5 minutes, turning once, until nicely browned on both sides. Remove from the oven and place on a baking rack to cool.

2 Heat the remaining stick of butter in a stock pot over medium heat. Cook the onions for 5 minutes, until they begin to turn translucent. Add the potatoes and cook for 5 more minutes over medium heat, stirring constantly. Add 1 cup chicken stock to the pot and stir well, scraping up any bits that have stuck to the bottom. Cook at a simmer, uncovered, for about 15 minutes, until the potatoes begin to soften. Add the remaining stock, the lemon juice, and black pepper to taste.

3 Add 2 cups of milk, reducing the heat to low and the pot to a slow simmer. Add the strained dill pickle brine and stir well. Puree the soup with an immersion blender or in batches in a food processor. Add the chopped pickles, dill, and chives, stirring to incorporate. If the soup is thicker than you like it at this point, add milk to taste. Cook for 5 more minutes over low heat, and turn off the heat. Serve in wide, deep bowls, topped with croutons and freshly ground black pepper.

KIMCHI RICE WITH BACON AND EGGS

From Sohui Kim, chef and co-owner of The Good Fork in Red Hook

This fast, simple Korean supper—a little salt, a little brine, a little fat, a little rice—is from chef Sohui Kim, who owns The Good Fork with her husband and makes vats of housemade pickled vegetables with her mother a few times a year, a process we captured in an issue of *Edible Brooklyn* along with this dish. It's not on The Good Fork's menu (there they pair their kimchi with steak), but it is what Kim makes at home. Now we do, too.

4 SLICES THICK-CUT BACON, CUT INTO 1-INCH PIECES
1 CUP PREPARED KIMCHI, THINLY SLICED
1 TSP SUGAR
2 TBSP RICE WINE VINEGAR
2–3 CUPS LEFTOVER RICE, PREFERABLY STEAMED SUSHI RICE
4 EGGS

Serves 2

1 Place the bacon in a cold sauté pan set over medium heat, and brown on both sides. Remove the cooked bacon and set aside. Pour out all but about 1 tablespoon of fat from the pan, reserving the rest to cook the eggs.

2 Cook the kimchi in the small amount of the reserved bacon fat for 5 minutes over medium heat until it's warmed through and sprinkle in the sugar and vinegar.

3 Fold in the rice and cooked bacon until evenly mixed and heated through, loosely cover with foil, and set aside.

4 In a small nonstick skillet, fry the eggs sunny-side up in a teaspoon or two of the balance of the bacon fat. Pile the kimchi rice mixture onto two plates and top with two eggs apiece. Serve hot.

BROOKLYN GREEN TOMATO CHUTNEY

*From Laena McCarthy,
owner of Anarchy in a Jar*

With a penchant for using local produce where she can, Laena McCarthy makes cutting-edge jams, jellies, preserves, and chutneys—sometimes delivering the goods to local customers by bicycle. The tomatoes McCarthy uses in this dish are "true urban tomatoes," she says, "grown with love and devotion by our friends at Brooklyn Grange Rooftop Farm in Long Island City, a one-acre urban farm. Many of these tomatoes were grown from seed in the greenhouses at Roberta's [pizzeria] in Bushwick, Brooklyn [see page 67] before being planted on the roof." McCarthy's green tomato chutney is also an eye-opener. "Green tomatoes may conjure the first frost and the sad end to summer's farm bounty," she says, "but they're also a way to preserve the perfect tang of summer—a flavor that can never be replicated by their inferior winter cousins, grown with hydroponics or in factory farms far away. Smear it on roast chicken, nibble it with toast, swirl some in your polenta, or enjoy alongside some perfectly poached eggs."

2 LB UNRIPE GREEN TOMATOES, FINELY DICED

1 CUP DICED ONIONS

½ CUP CURRANTS

2 SMALL HOT CHILE PEPPERS, STEMS AND SEEDS REMOVED, DICED

¼ CUP SWEET VERMOUTH

3 TBSP BROWN SUGAR

3 TBSP CIDER VINEGAR

2 TSP MUSTARD SEEDS

½ TSP CHILE PEPPER FLAKES

¼ TSP SMOKED PAPRIKA

SALT

¼ LB RED TOMATOES, FINELY DICED

Makes 6 pints

1 Combine the tomatoes, onions, currants, hot chile peppers, vermouth, brown sugar, vinegar, mustard seeds, chile pepper flakes, paprika, and salt to taste in a large saucepan, and bring to a boil over high heat. Reduce heat and simmer, uncovered, for 25 minutes. Add the red tomatoes.

2 Continue to simmer for about 1 hour, carefully stirring occasionally to keep the chutney from sticking to the pan and more frequently as the tomatoes soften and the texture thickens. When the mixture has thickened considerably and looks like chutney as opposed to tomato sauce, it's done. A good test is to pour a small spoonful onto a plate that has been kept in the freezer: the mixture should be jammy and spreadable.

3 Store the chutney in airtight glass or ceramic containers in the refrigerator for up to 1 month. (These jars could also be processed in a water bath so they will be shelf stable, says McCarthy. Immediately after the chutney is done, spoon into pre-sterilized canning jars and process in a boiling-water bath for 15 minutes.)

PICKLED RAMPS

*From Shamus Jones,
owner/founder of Brooklyn Brine*

Brooklyn pickler and pickling professor—he's just opened his own kitchen/studio to teach the rest of us how to put by—Shamus Jones has a great and simple tagline: "Damn Fine Pickles." His creations are locally sourced and seasonally inspired, and these two recipes are for early spring foods foraged in the forest—although you can get both from some farm stands or well-stocked specialty markets. "I have a black thumb and a fear of nature," jokes Jones, "so I leave that end up to the people who do it best." That's true: Jones gets his ramps from his friend Guy Jones of beloved Blooming Hill Farms in upstate New York. The brine used to pickle the ramps is a relatively traditional one, with the flavors of fennel seed and spicy red pepper adding a hot anise edge to the sweet oniony flavor of the bulbs.

1 GALLON WATER (PLUS EXTRA FOR STERILIZING JARS)
1 GALLON APPLE CIDER VINEGAR (5% ACIDITY)
1⅛ CUPS SEA SALT
¾ CUP EVAPORATED CANE SUGAR
5 LB RAMP BULBS, TRIMMED OF THEIR GREEN SHOOTS TO ABOUT 3 INCHES TALL, WASHED OF THEIR DIRT AND SAND

SPICES FOR EACH JAR:
½ TBSP CORIANDER SEED
½ TBSP YELLOW MUSTARD SEED
½ TSP FENNEL SEED
8–10 BLACK PEPPERCORNS
¼ TSP CRUSHED RED PEPPER

SPECIAL EQUIPMENT:
15 (8 OZ) JARS WITH LIDS
STAINLESS STEEL NONREACTIVE STOCK POT
JAR TONGS
WIDE-MOUTH FUNNEL

Makes 15 jars

1 Submerge the jars in a large stock pot filled with water, bring to a boil over high heat, and boil for 15 minutes. Remove the sterilized jars carefully with jar tongs and stand them upside down on a drying rack.

2 While the jars are being sterilized, make the brine by combining the gallon of water, vinegar, salt, and sugar in a large pot over medium-high heat. Bring to a boil. Boil for 3 minutes, reduce the heat, and simmer until the salt and sugar have dissolved. Keep warm.

3 Trim ⅛ inch off the end of each ramp bulb, peel away the thin outer layer of skin, and set the bulbs aside.

4 Place all the jar lids in the large stock pot filled with water, bring to a boil over high heat, and boil for 5 minutes. Remove them carefully with the lid tongs. Towel dry the sterilized jars and add the spices to each. Equally distribute the ramps among the jars.

5 Using a funnel, evenly distribute the brine among the jars to ⅛ to ¼ inch from the top. Wipe the outside thread of the jar with a clean towel, affix and tighten the lids, and, using jar tongs, submerge the jars in a large stock pot filled with water. Bring to a boil, and boil for 8 minutes.

6 Remove the jars from the pot. When cool enough to handle, check the button seal on the jar lids (see Edible Technique, opposite page). Label the jars, date them, and store in a cool, dark place for up to 6 months. Refrigerate after opening.

PICKLED FIDDLEHEAD FERNS

*From Shamus Jones,
owner/founder of Brooklyn Brine*

The fiddlehead brine is distinctly Asian and more layered, with the *umeboshi* (plum) vinegar taking the natural, slightly bitter edge off the ferns.

Edible Technique

To ensure that a processed jar is well sealed and can be stored without refrigeration, check the lid's button in its center: after a sealed jar has been removed from a water bath, that button should not pop up. If it does, depress the button, and turn the jar upside down; if it does not stay down when the jar is righted, change the lid and reprocess within 12 hours, or store in the refrigerator and use the fiddleheads within 1 week.

2 CUPS WATER (PLUS EXTRA FOR STERILIZING JARS)
2 CUPS UMEBOSHI VINEGAR
1⅛ CUP SALT
⅛ CUP CANE SUGAR
2 LB FIDDLEHEADS, ENDS TRIMMED, BLANCHED, AND SHOCKED THREE TIMES IN COLD WATER BATH
4-INCH PIECE OF GINGER, PEELED AND DICED
6 KAFFIR LIME LEAVES
2 STALKS LEMONGRASS, TRIMMED AND SLICED

SPICES FOR EACH JAR:
¼ TSP CORIANDER SEED
¼ TSP YELLOW MUSTARD SEED
⅛ TSP BLACK PEPPERCORNS
¼ TSP CRUSHED RED PEPPER

SPECIAL EQUIPMENT:
12 (8 OZ) JARS WITH LIDS
STAINLESS STEEL NONREACTIVE STOCK POT
JAR TONGS
WIDE-MOUTH FUNNEL

Makes 12 jars

1 Submerge the jars in a large stock pot filled with water, bring to a boil over high heat, and boil for 15 minutes. Remove the sterilized jars carefully with jar tongs and stand them upside down on a drying rack.

2 While the jars are being sterilized, make the brine by combining the 2 cups water, vinegar, salt, and sugar in a large pot over medium-high heat. Bring to a boil. Boil for 3 minutes, reduce the heat, and simmer until the salt and sugar have dissolved. Keep warm.

3 Trim ⅛ inch off the base of the stem of each fiddlehead, pat the fiddleheads dry, and set aside.

4 Place all the jar lids in the large stock pot filled with water, bring to a boil over high heat, and boil for 5 minutes. Remove them carefully with the lid tongs. Towel dry the sterilized jars and add the spices to each. Equally distribute the fiddleheads among the jars.

5 Using a funnel, evenly distribute the brine among the jars to ⅛ to ¼ inch from the top. Wipe the outside thread of the jar with a clean towel, affix and tighten the lids, and, using jar tongs, submerge the jars in a large stock pot filled with water. Bring to a boil, and boil for 8 minutes.

6 Remove the jars from the pot, and when cool enough to handle, check the button seal on the jar lids (see Edible Technique). Label the jars, date them, and store in a cool, dark place for up to 6 months. Refrigerate after opening.

THE BROOKLYN KITCHEN

Where Brooklyn foodies go to get real.

It is a happy fact that most of what is great and good in contemporary Brooklyn food—the concept that cooking from scratch is a noble pastime, the idea that good eating is a bedfellow with good politics, plus pork belly, malted barley, heirloom tomatoes, Bluebird kraut crocks, salted caramels, and the Sodastream Jet home soda maker—can be found at just one address: 100 Frost Street. There, practically under the Brooklyn-Queens Expressway in an old three-level rag shop still outfitted with a nineteenth-century cast-iron scale, lives The Brooklyn Kitchen, aka The Brooklyn Kitchen Labs, aka The Meat Hook.

The Kitchen started out with just one name in 2006. Then it was a tiny kitchenwares shop appropriately crammed with cast iron, cutting boards, and egg timers—"someone sets them off at least once a day," says co-owner Taylor Erkkinen—plus a small but critical collection of cookbooks and retro cookware. (The latter is largely the province of Erkkinen's husband and co-owner, Harry Rosenblum, thanks to his penchant for early morning estate sales.) Back then, Rosenblum was a lighting designer at Barnard College and Erkkinen was a construction project manager. Both loved to cook, but

there wasn't a place to buy what they wanted anywhere in Williamsburg. So the thirtysomething pair—both that rare combination of tough as nails and nurture—decided to open up their own.

The shoppers came, and they didn't respond just to the wares—each piece usually sold with a how-to from the owners, who practice the DIY curing, braising, and home brewing they preach—but to the classes in the basement, especially the pig butchery

101 taught by Tom Mylan. Mylan wasn't yet a household name among offal obsessives, but still a butcher in training, literally learning on the job (and with a monthlong stint upstate at Fleischer's Grass-Fed and Organic Meats) when the two sister restaurants he then worked for—Diner and Marlowe & Sons—started buying whole animals from local small farms and selling the meat.

Mylan helped launch Marlowe's successful butcher shop, but when The Brooklyn Kitchen decided to expand,

The Meat Hook—home to housemade pâtés, terrines, house-aged steaks, cured hams, lamb heads, vats of demiglace, and about two dozens kinds of sausages you'll most likely never see anywhere else—was born. Along with it came The Brooklyn Kitchen Labs, a pair of classrooms designed to accommodate the sold-out courses (knife sharpening, piecrusts, Christmas cookies, canning, cured fish, Chinese dumplings) and meet-ups (book clubs, home brewers, bread bakers, farm activist fundraisers) The Brooklyn Kitchen hosts nearly every night.

Better still, in between the two are yards of the extra space earmarked for more cookbooks and kitchen supplies, which have expanded to include local dairy products, eggs, and Pennsylvania Amish country produce kept in a fat-handled old fridge, bulk grain bins, and olive oils, home-brewing supplies, spices, sauces, Brooklyn canned goods and chocolate bars, vinegars, extracts from orange to vanilla, and, last but not least, one life-size cow painted graffiti style with the Statue of Liberty.

And while you can't quite yet fully live at 100 Frost Street, we suspect if they ever offered sleepaway cooking camp, we wouldn't be the first folks in line.

PICKLED HERRING AND POTATO SALAD WITH CRÈME FRAÎCHE AND DILL

From Peter Berley, chef

A James Beard award–winning author for his cookbook *The Modern Vegetarian Kitchen*, local chef Peter Berley was one of the first in the country to marry a sustainable outlook with killer culinary instincts. His sublime homemade pizzas, for example, are chewy-crusted delights, often topped with home-fermented kraut from farmers' market cabbage, a dollop of just-made yogurt, and bacon cured in Brooklyn. This dish—which appeared in an *Edible Brooklyn* story about how to be a winter locavore—is just as wonderful. Berley buys pickled herring—tiny, oily fish that are pickled or smoked throughout Eastern Europe—and tosses them with the earthy creaminess of fingerling potatoes, the tart richness of crème fraîche, and the brightness of lemon and dill. This recipe, which Berley calls "northern European peasant food," is simple to make, and since it's served cold and can be made up to 3 hours ahead, it's an ideal starter for a dinner party in winter or early spring.

2 LB FINGERLING POTATOES, SCRUBBED
3 (12 OZ) JARS PICKLED HERRING
2 CUPS CRÈME FRAÎCHE
1 LEMON, ZEST FINELY GRATED AND JUICE FRESHLY SQUEEZED
¼ CUP CHOPPED FRESH DILL, PLUS SPRIGS FOR GARNISH
SALT
CRACKED BLACK PEPPER

Serves 8–10

1 Place the potatoes in a large pot with salted water to cover and bring to a boil. Cook until tender (about 15 minutes). Drain and let rest until cool enough to handle. Slip potatoes from their skins and slice into ½-inch-thick rounds.

2 Drain the pickled herring, reserving about ½ cup of the brine. In a large bowl, toss the herring with the potatoes, crème fraîche, lemon zest and juice, and chopped dill. Drizzle with a little of the reserved brine and add salt and pepper to taste. Refrigerate until chilled.

3 Serve garnished with sprigs of dill.

Edible Tip

For this dish, Berley buys Blue Hill Bay from Acme Smoked Fish, a fourth-generation Brooklyn business that's the country's largest producer of smoked fish and herring, all hot- or cold-smoked the old-fashioned way, without chemicals. If you can't find the brand in your local supermarket, you can always plan a trip to their Greenpoint retail shop.

CORA'S BROCCOLI SALAD

*From Joe Carroll, co-owner of
Fette Sau, Spuyten Duyvil bar
and Spuyten Duyvil Grocery,
and St. Anselm*

1   LB BROCCOLI, STALKS REMOVED
    AND FLORETS BROKEN OR
    CUT INTO BITE-SIZE PIECES
¼   CUP FRESH LEMON JUICE
¾   CUP EXTRA-VIRGIN OLIVE OIL
2   CLOVES GARLIC, FINELY MINCED

CHILE PEPPER FLAKES
SALT
FRESHLY GROUND BLACK PEPPER

Serves 4–6

Joe and Kim Carroll's businesses follow Joe's culinary passions, and it's served them well. His first Brooklyn business, named after a creek in the Bronx, quickly became one of the best places for craft brews in the country. He's also an avid backyard barbecuer, and his restaurant Fette Sau (German for "fat pig") is consistently ranked best barbecue in the New York City *Zagat Guide*. We love Fette's draft beer and Bourbon lists and its house-smoked brisket, but a meal isn't complete without the lemony tang of Joe's broccoli salad, created by Joe's Italian grandmother, a Bronxite named Cora.

1 Bring ¾ to 1 inch of water to a boil in a saucepan lined with a steamer. Steam the broccoli florets until they turn bright green and just barely begin to soften. Remove from heat and set aside in a large bowl.

2 Whisk together the lemon juice and olive oil until they emulsify. Mix in the garlic.

3 Pour the lemon-juice mixture on top of the broccoli, toss, add the chile flakes, salt, and pepper to taste, and toss again to mix together. Serve cold or at room temperature.

CAULIFLOWER TWO WAYS

*From Catherine Saillard,
iCi restaurant in Fort Greene*

This cauliflower dish appeared in the pages of *Edible Brooklyn* in 2007 and is so beloved it's been on the menu at iCi restaurant—one of brownstone Brooklyn's long-standing destinations for locavores— in some form since it opened in 2004. It's a knockout of a side, one of those rare creations that'll make you rethink a vegetable, in this case, cauliflower. Follow the lead of iCi owner, Catherine Saillard, and pair it with her Braised Pork Shoulder with Cider Vinegar, Whole-Grain Mustard, and Brown Beer (page 59).

2 HEADS CAULIFLOWER,
   BROKEN INTO FLORETS, CORE
   REMOVED AND CUT IN HALF
½ GALLON MILK
SALT

½ LB UNSALTED BUTTER
½ CUP PINE NUTS
FRESHLY GROUND BLACK PEPPER

Serves 6–8

1 Set about a third of the florets aside. Transfer the remaining cauliflower and the core halves to a stock pot, cover with the milk, and heat to a simmer. Cook till cauliflower is soft, about 12 minutes. Drain, reserving half of the liquid.

2 When cool enough to handle, transfer the cooked cauliflower to a blender and process with some of the reserved liquid until just pureed. Do not add too much liquid or it will be too thin. Season with salt to taste.

3 Melt the butter in a large saucepan over high heat and sauté the reserved florets, uncovered, until browned, about 5 minutes. Add the pine nuts and continue to cook over medium heat for about 3 minutes. Season with salt and pepper to taste.

4 Serve the puree topped with the florets and pine nuts.

BLACK-EYED PEAS

From Amelia Coulter,
owner of Sugarbuilt

Brooklyn is full of transplants, many of whom rekindle a connection to their native foods after they move away from home. That's true of this spicy dish from Amelia Coulter, an artist and Brooklyn sugar-cookie baker known for the intricate designs she paints with icing. As a kid growing up in New Mexico, Coulter hated black-eyed peas (which are in fact not peas, but legumes), but now the once-dreaded holiday food—eaten along with collard greens for good luck on New Year's across the South and Southwest—have taken on new meaning. "Now black-eyed peas have become a food I dearly love and am sincerely superstitious about." These have one thing most Southerners don't, however, and that's plenty of spicy green peppers. "The New Mexican in me," says Coulter, who uses both dried and canned beans, giving the dish a layered texture, "will only feel reassured if there is green chile added." This recipe makes enough for a (large) holiday crowd.

½ LB SLICED BACON, CUT IN HALF CROSSWISE INTO BATONS
2 LARGE ONIONS, CHOPPED
4 CLOVES GARLIC, CHOPPED
4 OZ PROSCIUTTO, DICED
1 16 OZ BAG DRY BLACK-EYED PEAS, SOAKED OVERNIGHT AND DRAINED
2 15 OZ CANS BLACK-EYED PEAS, DRAINED
1 BAY LEAF
¼ CUP WHITE WINE

2 CUPS CHICKEN STOCK
2 TBSP RICE WINE VINEGAR, PREFERABLY BROWN
2 CUPS CANNED GREEN CHILES OR ROASTED, PEELED, AND SEEDED FRESH NEW MEXICAN GREEN HATCH CHILES
SALT
FRESHLY GROUND BLACK PEPPER

Serves a crowd (about 30) as a side

1 In a large, heavy pot with a lid cook the bacon over medium-high heat until the edges just begin to brown. Add the onions and garlic, and sauté until translucent. Add the prosciutto and cook until it just begins to brown, 3–4 minutes.

2 Add the black-eyed peas and bay leaf, and cover with white wine, stock, and vinegar, adding water if the liquid doesn't cover the contents of the pot. Cover and cook over medium-high heat, reducing the heat if it starts to boil over, for 15–20 minutes. Reduce the heat slightly and add the green chiles and the salt and pepper to taste.

3 Continue to simmer uncovered for 15–30 minutes more, tasting from time to time and adding salt and pepper, if needed, until the soaked peas are cooked through and tender. (The canned peas will be a little mushier, but that's okay.)

ROASTED SWEET POTATOES
WITH FRIED LEEKS AND PARMESAN

*From Christy Harrison,
food writer and master's candidate
in food studies at NYU*

A former online editor for *Gourmet.com*, Christy Harrison often makes these roasted sweet potatoes—dressed up with frizzled leeks and a wash of salty Parmesan cheese—for dinner on their own, and they'd be a great addition to the winter repertoire of any locavoric-minded eater. (They also pair perfectly with a Szechuan-spiced brisket Harrison created, page 78.)

4 LARGE SWEET POTATOES, PEELED AND CUT INTO ½-INCH CUBES
5 TBSP OLIVE OIL
SALT
FRESHLY GROUND BLACK PEPPER
4 LARGE LEEKS (WHITE PARTS ONLY), CLEANED, QUARTERED, AND SLICED INTO ⅛-INCH RIBBONS

½ CUP PARMESAN CHEESE, FINELY GRATED
JUICE FROM 1 MEDIUM LIME

Serves 6

1 Preheat the oven to 450°F.

2 Toss the sweet potatoes in 2 tablespoons of the olive oil and sprinkle lightly with salt. Spread the potatoes in a single layer on one large cookie sheet or sheet pan and roast, uncovered, rotating the pan halfway through roasting, about 15–20 minutes total. The potatoes should be fork-tender and the undersides should be browned.

3 While the potatoes are roasting, heat the remaining 3 tablespoons oil in a large skillet over medium-high heat until shimmering. Add the leeks and sauté, stirring frequently, until they begin to brown, about 4–5 minutes. Remove from the heat, transfer to a large serving bowl, and set aside.

4 When the potatoes are done roasting, remove from the oven and place the pan on a wire rack. Loosen the potatoes with a spatula and allow them to cool slightly, about 5 minutes.

5 Transfer the potatoes to the serving bowl with the leeks and toss with the Parmesan and lime juice. Add salt and pepper to taste. Serve immediately.

RAW KALE SALAD WITH PEANUT-HONEY DRESSING

*From Stacey Murphy,
founder of BK Farmyards*

As the founder of BK Farmyards, Stacey Murphy has proven not just that you can farm in the city, but that you can do it without even owning any land. By growing crops or raising chickens or honeybees on a network of tiny Brooklyn parcels—backyards, empty lots, and corners of community gardens—Murphy's "farming network" supplied both a 6-person CSA and a weekly farm stand, providing employment and education to local kids in the process. This raw kale salad became a favorite of vegetable-scorning high-school kids Murphy worked with on a Summer Youth Employment Program, so you know it's got to be good.

1 LARGE BUNCH OF KALE
   (ABOUT 12–15 STALKS), WASHED
   AND CUT INTO ¼-INCH STRIPS
JUICE FROM 3 LEMONS
   (ABOUT 5 TBSP)
¼ CUP WHITE WINE VINEGAR
¼ CUP EXTRA-VIRGIN OLIVE OIL
2 TBSP HONEY

2 TBSP NATURAL SMOOTH PEANUT
   BUTTER (NO SUGAR ADDED)
¼ CUP SESAME SEEDS
SALT
FRESHLY GROUND BLACK PEPPER

Serves 4

1 Place the kale in a large glass or stainless steel bowl, pour the lemon juice and vinegar over it, and toss well. Let sit for 3 minutes to tenderize the greens.

2 In medium bowl, whisk the olive oil, honey, and peanut butter to combine. Pour over the kale, using a spatula to scrape down the sides of the bowl if needed.

3 Sprinkle with the sesame seeds and salt and pepper to taste. Mix well.

RADISHES SAUTÉED WITH CREAM AND HERBS

*From Diner restaurant
in Williamsburg*

The following recipe was created by chef Carolina Fidanza (see profile, page 10) for Diner and appeared in *Edible Brooklyn*'s fifth issue, in an ode to the space she helped found. Diner is one of Brooklyn's seminal restaurants and also one of its most beautiful, thanks to the namesake silver dining car and corner spot under the Williamsburg Bridge just a block from the waterfront and just next door to its sister spot, a wine bar called Marlowe & Sons. Most folks would never dream of cooking a radish, but they cook up like turnips and are twice as tasty in this clever spring side. If you can't find scapes, the twirly green tops of young garlic that appear at markets in spring, use regular garlic cloves.

2 TBSP UNSALTED BUTTER
2 TBSP EXTRA-VIRGIN OLIVE OIL
2 TBSP GREEN GARLIC SCAPES, SLICED, OR USE 1 TBSP MINCED GARLIC
2 LARGE BUNCHES RADISHES, CLEANED AND QUARTERED
SALT
½ CUP CHICKEN STOCK OR WATER

2 TBSP HEAVY CREAM
1 BUNCH CHIVES, CUT INTO ¼-INCH SLICES
1 BUNCH SCALLIONS, THINLY SLICED ON THE BIAS
FRESHLY GROUND BLACK PEPPER

Serves 4–6

1 Heat the butter together with the olive oil in a skillet over high heat until shimmering. Add the garlic scapes or fine-minced garlic cloves and cook until soft, 1–2 minutes.

2 Add the radishes to the pan, season with salt, and cook another minute or two, until they begin to brown. Pour in the stock, reduce the heat, and simmer until the radishes are tender, 2–3 minutes.

3 Add the cream, increase the heat to high, and cook until the cream thickens and clings to the radishes, about 1 minute. Toss in the chives and scallions, and season with salt and pepper to taste. Serve immediately.

KOHL SLAW FROM ANOTHER PLANET

From Jennifer Prediger, writer/ humorist/video producer for Grist.org

In addition to her day job for the environmental website Grist, Jennifer Prediger pens an advice column and blogs about what she does with her weekly haul from one of Brooklyn's many CSAs. "I wish I could say I got this recipe from my German grandmother Prediger," she says, but "a farm-fresh display of intergalactic-looking vegetables caught my eye one day over the summer at the Carroll Gardens Greenmarket. Those imagination-grabbing vegetables were kohlrabi (technically the swollen stem of a plant related to wild cabbage), fall garlic scapes nearly in bloom, and white turnips. I asked the cute hipster boy farmer from upstate what one could do with such awe-inspiring vegetables. He said they made a great cole (kohl) slaw."

2–3 FALL HARD-NECK GARLIC SCAPES (INCLUDING BULBS AND TOPS; SEE EDIBLE TIP), OR USE 2–3 SCALLIONS, WHITE AND VERY LIGHT GREEN PARTS ONLY, CHOPPED

1 LARGE KOHLRABI, GREEN OR PURPLE, SCRUBBED AND PEELED

2 LARGE OR 3 SMALL WHITE TURNIPS, SCRUBBED AND PEELED

3–4 TBSP MAYONNAISE

SALT

FRESHLY GROUND BLACK PEPPER

Makes 1 quart

1 Peel the papery outer layer off the bulbs from the tops of the garlic scapes (depending on how large they are). Finely mince the tops and bulbs.

2 Slice the kohlrabi and the turnips thinly using the large-holed side of a box grater or a mandoline.

3 Toss the vegetables together in a large bowl. Add mayonnaise, salt, and pepper to taste and toss again to mix.

Edible Tip

In the fall, some hard-stem garlic varieties—known as top-setting garlic—produce beautiful scapes crowned with round flowering pods containing tiny garlic bulbs that can themselves be planted. Farmers fold the stalks over and cover them with soil, but you can also eat them and enjoy their lovely mild flavor. Just open up the pods—"lots of little purple pearls will spill out," says Prediger—clean them of their papery outer shells, and mince them like regular cloves.

LIZA'S STATE-FAIR SALT POTATOES

From Liza Queen,
former chef of Queen's Hideaway

Until she lost her lease—which broke many Brooklyn hearts—Liza Queen ran a self-named spot in a sliver of a space next door to her apartment, letting diners eat in her backyard patio, filled with herbs and plants. She cooked what she wanted—pulled pork, hush puppies, tomato salads, Dutch pancakes—played records on a real stereo, and set pies on her back windowsill to cool. "My first job was making salt potatoes at the state fair," the upstate New York native told us when we profiled her in an early issue of *Edible Brooklyn*. "They're the easiest things in the universe. They're a full-on Syracuse State Fair staple. Now all you need is an ear of corn and a steak and you have my favorite summer meal of all time."

5 LB CLEANED POTATOES, IDEALLY GERMAN BUTTERBALL OR YUKON GOLD

3 CUPS KOSHER SALT

1½ STICKS BUTTER, CUT INTO ½-INCH SLICES

Serves 10

1 Put the potatoes in a large stock pot filled with enough cold water to cover them by a few inches. Pour half of the salt into the pot and stir well. Continue pouring in more salt (it will seem like more than you think you'll need), and stir until it has dissolved and the potatoes float. If they don't float, add more salt. Bring the water to a boil over high heat.

2 Reduce the heat and simmer until the potatoes are tender when pierced with a fork, about 12–15 minutes.

3 Drain the potatoes, and serve immediately in a bowl topped with butter.

LOCAL POLE BEAN SALAD

*From Francine Stephens and
Andrew Feinberg of Franny's and
Brooklyn Larder in Prospect Heights*

A few years after founding Franny's, their beloved modern pizzeria and Italian restaurant on Flatbush Avenue, Francine Stephens and Andrew Feinberg (page 97) decided to open up a grocery, stocking many of the wonderful cheeses, olive oils, meats, pastas, pickles, and chocolate Feinberg used in Franny's kitchen. They also decided to serve plenty of fantastic food to go—fat slices of lasagna, a sandwich of oil-slicked lemony greens and warm ricotta, and red-sauce-soaked meatballs, to name a few. This essence-of-summer bean salad might sound ridiculously simple at first, but the just barely sweet, barely spicy blend of champagne vinegar and great-quality oil (Stephens recommends Frantoia), and very detailed cooking method, show off the couple's supreme skills at highlighting fine ingredients, and it's ultimately so good we asked for the recipe pronto. You don't have to snap the beans, but do make sure you've removed any rough bits of stem.

2   TBSP MINCED SHALLOTS
2   TBSP CHAMPAGNE VINEGAR
⅓   CUP EXTRA-VIRGIN OLIVE OIL
    ICE, FOR BATH
¼   CUP KOSHER SALT, PLUS MORE
    AS DESIRED

1   LB WHOLE FRESH SUMMER
    BEANS, SUCH AS YELLOW WAX
    BEANS, GREEN BEANS, OR
    ROMANO BEANS, TIPPED
    AND TAILED
    FRESHLY GROUND BLACK PEPPER

Serves 4–6

1 In a glass jar with a tight lid, shake together the shallots, vinegar, and olive oil, and set aside.

2 Bring a large pot of water to a rolling boil over high heat. Meanwhile, prepare an ice-water bath of 50 percent ice and 50 percent water in a large bowl.

3 Add the salt to the boiling water and give it a taste (it should taste like seawater, and you may need to add more than ¼ cup). Add the beans in batches, a handful at a time, and cook each batch for 1–3 minutes, tasting as you go, until they retain just a slight crunch. The beans should always be moving very freely and the water should not stop boiling at any point.

4 Remove the beans from the water and rest them in the ice bath for several minutes, until they cool, adding the beans from subsequent batches as you go. You may need to add more ice as it melts.

5 Drain the beans and allow them to dry, spreading them out on a kitchen towel to remove any excess water. When the beans are cool, slice them into 1- to 2-inch pieces and place in a medium bowl.

6 Dress the beans with the vinaigrette to taste (you should have a bit left over to reserve for your next salad) and pepper to taste, adding a pinch more salt if needed.

BROOKLYN LARDER, PROSPECT HEIGHTS

CHAPTER 3

MAINS

Long before celebrity butchers hit the Style
pages, Brooklyn was obsessed with proteins and blessed with the best.
Skilled butchers have always been fixtures here: third-generation Italian
and Polish pork stores make sausages for your supper alongside farmers
raising some of the country's most excellent meats and fishmongers with
briny oysters, sweet scallops, and bluefish procured just a short drive away.
A Brooklyn beer-braised pork-roast recipe is stellar, in other words; our
scallops with fast lemon sauce fantastic; our weeknight sage-roasted chicken
simply awesome. And should you be vegetarian, no worry: we make some
of the country's best mac and cheese as well as fresh tofu, handmade in
Brooklyn's own Chinatown.

BRAISED PORK SHOULDER WITH CIDER VINEGAR, WHOLE-GRAIN MUSTARD, AND BROWN BEER

*From Catherine Saillard,
owner of iCi restaurant*

"I am not much of a cook," admits Catherine Saillard, owner of iCi, one of brownstone Brooklyn's loveliest places to eat. But, she says, "this is foolproof." Like her restaurant, this dish is "juicy and delicious" and is inspired by what's available locally, either from farmers' markets or from the nearby urban farm called Added Value, which supplies much of iCi's salad greens. For best results, Saillard recommends seeking out Brooklyn-brewed beer and sustainably raised pork—especially from Flying Pigs Farm, the upstate New York farm that sells in Brooklyn on Saturdays and through *FlyingPigsFarm.com*—and serving it with cauliflower and sautéed kale. Don't worry about adding too much oil and fat to the pan when you brown the meat, says Saillard: "I am French," she laughs, "and I'm not afraid of butter."

3–4 LB BONELESS PORK SHOULDER, TRIMMED OF FAT
SALT
FRESHLY GROUND BLACK PEPPER
5 TBSP EXTRA-VIRGIN OLIVE OIL
2 TBSP UNSALTED BUTTER
1 MEDIUM CARROT, CHOPPED
1 MEDIUM ONION, CHOPPED
3 STALKS CELERY, CHOPPED
12 OZ DARK BROWN BEER (SUCH AS BROOKLYN BREWERY'S BROOKLYN BROWN ALE)
4 BAY LEAVES
LEAVES FROM 5 SPRIGS FRESH THYME
1 JALAPEÑO, WHOLE, POKED WITH THE TINES OF A FORK
1 WHOLE HEAD GARLIC, UNPEELED CUT IN HALF LENGTHWISE
5 MEDIUM TOMATOES, QUARTERED
½ CUP CIDER VINEGAR
½ CUP WHOLE-GRAIN MUSTARD
1½ QT CHICKEN STOCK OR 1 QT STOCK AND 2 CUPS WATER

Serves 6–8

1 Preheat the oven to 350°F. Season the pork shoulder with salt and pepper to taste.

2 Heat the oil and butter together in a large enameled, cast-iron Dutch oven until shimmering. Sear the meat on all sides until golden brown. Remove and set aside while you sauté the vegetables.

3 Sauté the carrot, onion, and celery in the Dutch oven over medium heat until soft and lightly caramelized. Add the beer, increase the heat slightly, and scrape up all of the caramelized bits stuck to the bottom of the pan. Move the vegetables to the sides of the pot and place the pork back into the center. Add the bay leaves, thyme, jalapeño, garlic, tomatoes, vinegar, mustard, and stock to the pot. Cover with a tight-fitting lid and place in the oven. Braise for 2–3 hours or until tender, checking the pot several times to make sure it is not drying out, and adding more stock or water if it is.

4 Transfer the pork to a cutting board, loosely drape with foil, and let rest for 10 minutes. Strain out the vegetables and discard. Reduce the braising liquid over high heat until it's syrupy, slice the meat against the grain, and serve with the sauce.

GREEN CHILI WITH BRAISED PORK, CRÈME FRAÎCHE, AND FETA

From Bret Macris, executive chef at Rose Water Restaurant in Park Slope

Long before *locavore* was a household word, Rose Water restaurant was showcasing local farms and seasonal cooking through its Pan-Mediterranean menu, which is as beloved by locals as is its wraparound sidewalk seating and romantic little dining room. This recipe, recently served at a fall fund-raiser for a local nonprofit that helps support urban farming, is actually inspired by both Mexico and the Mediterranean, though it's technically from Minneapolis. That's where Macris's in-laws make this addictive slow-cooked pork chili with friends as an excuse to socialize. While the chef has given us the stovetop method (his in-laws roast the peppers outside), you could try it backyard style too. "When it's all put together, the pot goes on top of the grill and stays there until it's done and we grill our own flatbread," says Macris. Even cooked indoors, this dish is still a fine reason to invite over friends. You could even let them plunge their freshly toasted tortillas straight into the pot. If you have leftovers, follow Macris's lead: "For breakfast, we'll poach an egg in it," he says, "or we'll use it as pizza topping too."

Edible Tip

If you want to go easy on the heat in this dish, omit the serrano pepper; if heat is what you're after, don't remove the seeds or ribs after you roast the peppers.

6 LARGE GREEN BELL PEPPERS, OR 8 GOOD-SIZE ANAHEIM OR OTHER MILD GREEN CHILE PEPPERS
2 JALAPEÑOS
1 SERRANO PEPPER (OPTIONAL)
2 TBSP VEGETABLE OIL
3 LB PORK SHOULDER OR PORK BUTT, TRIMMED OF MOST BUT NOT ALL OF THE FAT, CUBED
2 MEDIUM YELLOW ONIONS, THINLY SLICED
1 (12 OZ) BOTTLE OF YOUR FAVORITE LAGER
1 HEAD GARLIC, PEELED AND FINELY CHOPPED
2 CUPS LOW-SODIUM CHICKEN OR VEGETABLE BROTH
SALT
FRESHLY GROUND BLACK PEPPER
1 CUP CRÈME FRAÎCHE, LIGHTLY WHIPPED
1 CUP CRUMBLED FETA
FLATBREAD OR TORTILLAS, WARMED

Serves 6

1 Preheat the broiler. Place all the peppers in a broiler pan, and completely char them, rotating them often. When the skins are blackened and puffy, carefully place the peppers in an airtight container and let them sit for about 20 minutes. Peel off the charred skin, remove their stems and pull out the seeds and ribs, and reserve and strain any of the liquid that's left behind.

2 Heat the oil in a large, heavyweight pot set over medium-high heat until it shimmers. Working in batches, brown the pork until it begins to caramelize and releases most of its fat. Strain out the pork and set aside. Discard all but 2 tablespoons of the fat, and add the sliced onions to the pot. Reduce the heat to medium, and cook until the onions are caramelized and have turned a light golden brown. Add the beer and the garlic, simmering over medium-low heat until the liquid is reduced and thickened. Scrape the pan frequently as the liquid reduces.

3 Once the beer has reduced almost entirely, spoon out the onions with half of the peppers and their reserved liquid into the bowl of a food processor, and process until smooth. Place in a bowl, and set aside. Put the remainder of the peppers in the food processor and process until just chunky.

4 Add the chunky peppers and the onion and pepper puree back to the pot along with the pork and its juices, and simmer over medium-low heat. If the mixture is fairly thick, thin it out with some of the chicken stock to a more chili-like consistency. Cook for at least another hour, or until the pork is very tender. Season with salt and pepper to taste, serve topped with crème fraîche and feta, and pass flatbread or tortillas.

BEER-CAN CHICKEN

*From Steve Hindy,
co-founder, Brooklyn Brewery*

A former war correspondent for the Associated Press who learned how to home brew beer while living in the alcohol-free Middle East, Steve Hindy (see profile, page 66) learned this recipe in Italy, where he met North Carolina barbecue master Jim "Trim" Tabb at a Slow Food festival. "The first step in making beer-can chicken is in many ways the most fun," says Hindy. "You open a can of Brooklyn Lager and drink half of it. I buy my chickens at Meat Hook in Williamsburg and I roll them in rock salt and then stick sprigs of sage and thyme in the cavity and under the wings. (If you are not into salt, substitute fresh lemon juice and stick the lemon in the cavity and under the wings along with the herbs.) It is possible to balance the chicken on the grill, but there are stainless-steel stands available to hold the can and chicken upright. I put the chicken in a drip tray so the chicken fat does not ignite the grill. I also put potatoes, beets, and parsnips in the drip tray to stew in the schmaltzy juices. The vapors from the beer yield a moist and tasty chicken. I recommend you drink at least another can of Brooklyn Lager while the chicken cooks."

1 LARGE WHOLE CHICKEN (4–5 LB)
COARSELY GROUND SALT
5 SPRINGS ROSEMARY
5 SPRINGS SAGE
5 SPRINGS THYME
1 (12 OZ) CAN LAGER BEER,
    HALF-FULL

SPECIAL EQUIPMENT:
STAINLESS STEEL ROASTING STAND
    FOR BEER–CAN CHICKEN

Serves 4

1 Prepare a medium fire on a gas or charcoal grill with a cover.

2 Pat the chicken dry and rub the skin with salt. Place the herbs inside the cavity of the bird, sticking a few under the wings. Insert the half-full can of beer, open end up, into the abdominal cavity of the bird.

3 Using a stainless-steel roasting stand made for beer-can chicken, insert the chicken on the stand, cavity side down, over a tray to catch the drips.

4 Place the chicken on the grill and cover, roasting for at least an hour. If using a charcoal grill, you may need to add more coals to keep the grill at a medium fire. If you have a large gas grill, you could try Hindy's approach and cook the chicken on a higher temperature at the start: "For a 4-pound chicken, I turn all three burners on high for the first 15–20 minutes to cook the skin a nice golden brown. Then I turn off the middle burner and turn the others down to medium for the next hour."

5 Remove the chicken from the grill when done—juices will run clear and a thermometer inserted into the thickest part of the thigh will reach 160–165°F. Loosely tent with foil and let stand for 8 minutes before carving.

CAST-IRON CHICKEN WITH BACON AND SAUERKRAUT

From Harry Rosenblum and Taylor Erkkinen, co-owners of The Brooklyn Kitchen

As the couple behind what has to be Brooklyn's most beloved kitchen store and cooking school (see profile, page 42), Harry Rosenblum and Taylor Erkkinen are the type of cooks skilled at blending recipes from many sources and making use of what they have on hand—which in this case includes a Bulgarian chicken recipe, a primo bird from their in-house butcher shop, and an eleven-pound bag of carrots that literally fell off a produce truck. After reading a tweet about the drop from Eagle Street Rooftop's farmer Annie Novak (see page 15), who passed it en route to work— "Major spill of produce at Williamsburg and Kent streets!"—Rosenblum grabbed the bag and decided to make a ginger-carrot kraut. He and Taylor ended up with gallons of the stuff and eventually used it in this brilliant Eastern European–inflected dish, made all the more wonderful with the addition of bacon and smoked paprika. You don't have to make your own kraut for the dish, but if you do, rest assured you can buy all the equipment you need at The Brooklyn Kitchen.

½ LB SLAB BACON, DICED
1 WHOLE (3–4 LB) CHICKEN, QUARTERED
SALT
FRESHLY GROUND BLACK PEPPER
1 LARGE OR 2 SMALL ONIONS, CHOPPED
VEGETABLE OIL, IF NECESSARY

2 SMALL SPRIGS THYME
1 BAY LEAF
1 TSP CRUSHED RED PEPPER FLAKES
1 TSP SWEET SMOKED PAPRIKA
1 LB SAUERKRAUT
½ CUP CHICKEN STOCK OR WATER

Serves 4

1 Preheat the oven to 350°F.

2 Render the fat from the bacon in a large cast-iron skillet or ovenproof pan set over medium heat. Remove the bacon and set aside.

3 Season the chicken with salt and pepper to taste on all sides, and brown in the bacon fat. Transfer to a plate. Brown the onions in bacon fat, adding a bit of oil if necessary. Add the thyme, bay leaf, red pepper flakes, and paprika, and sauté briefly. Return the bacon to the pan and stir to mix in. Add the sauerkraut to the pan and stir to mix. Arrange the chicken pieces around the top of the pan on top of the sauerkraut and add the stock.

4 Transfer the pan to the oven and roast the chicken, uncovered, for about 40 minutes, checking the chicken pieces for doneness after 30 minutes. (If the pan begins to dry out, add a bit more stock.) The chicken is cooked when the juices run clear and an instant-read thermometer inserted into the thickest part of the thigh reads 165°F. Serve the chicken immediately with plenty of sauerkraut and pan juices.

FRESH TAGLIATELLE WITH SMOKED RICOTTA, LOCAL SWEET CORN, SUMMER CHANTERELLES, AND TARRAGON

From Saul Bolton, chef and owner of Saul and The Vanderbilt

In addition to being one of Brooklyn's most lauded chef-restaurateurs, Saul Bolton is also a pioneer. Saul, Bolton's fine French-inflected (he cheffed at Bouley in Manhattan before opening his own Brooklyn kitchen in 1999), seasonally inspired restaurant on Smith Street is the lynchpin of an established restaurant row and of the local farm-to-table movement. ("It's not who you are; it's how you're raised," he told us in the second issue of *Edible Manhattan*. "It's the same with pigs and carrots as it is with kids.") And The Vanderbilt, his new, more casual cocktail bar-cum-tavern (a lengthy drink and beer list, charcuterie, housemade sausages, and vegetable-driven small plates), was one of the first to move into an up-and-coming dining street in Prospect Heights. This summer pasta is based on a ricotta ravioli Bolton makes, reworked to provide home cooks with the same comforting blend of flavors. It's easier, of course, if you substitute store-bought tagliatelle.

1 WHOLE EGG
7 EGG YOLKS
2 TBSP EXTRA-VIRGIN OLIVE OIL
⅛ TSP SALT, PLUS MORE TO TASTE
2 CUPS ALL-PURPOSE FLOUR
6 TBSP BUTTER
½ LB SUMMER CHANTERELLES, BRUSHED LIGHTLY TO REMOVE ANY DIRT OR GRIT, OR SUBSTITUTE ANY FRESH MUSHROOM
4 MINCED SHALLOTS
1 CLOVE GARLIC, MINCED

1 TSP FRESH THYME LEAVES
4 EARS SWEET CORN, KERNELS REMOVED FROM THE COB
20 FRESH TARRAGON LEAVES
½ CUP GRATED PECORINO ROMANO CHEESE
¼ LB SMOKED FRESH RICOTTA, AT ROOM TEMPERATURE, OR SUBSTITUTE PLAIN RICOTTA
FRESHLY GROUND BLACK PEPPER

Serves 4

1 In a bowl combine the egg, egg yolks, olive oil, and ⅛ teaspoon salt.

2 Place the flour in the bowl of a food processor and pulse once or twice. Add the egg mixture and pulse until the flour absorbs the liquid. When you pinch it with your fingers, it should form a clump that's not too wet and not sticky but not too dry. If it's too wet, add 2 tablespoons of flour and pulse. If it feels too dry, add 2 tablespoons of water and pulse until smooth and moist to the touch.

3 Turn the dough out onto a lightly floured board and knead for 5 minutes. Using a sharp knife, slice the dough into four pieces. Using a pasta machine, roll each piece out until you can pass it through the thinnest setting and the resulting sheets are paper-thin. To cut the dough, pass it through the wide pasta blade. If you don't have a pasta machine, substitute 1 pound of best-quality fresh tagliatelle.

Edible Technique

Instead of mincing his garlic, chef Bolton sometimes simply grates it using a Microplane grater. It's an incredibly fast and easy shortcut that you'll turn to again and again when making dinner on a weeknight. Try grating the cloves right into dish when it comes time to add the garlic.

4 Bring a large sauce pot filled with salted water to a boil and cook the pasta until al dente, about 6 minutes. Stir frequently to make sure it is not sticking together as it cooks.

5 While the pasta is cooking, heat 3 tablespoons of the butter in a large sauté pan over medium-high heat. Add the chanterelles and cook until soft, about 2 minutes. Add the shallots and garlic, mix well, and cook for 1 minute. Add the thyme leaves and cook for another 30 seconds. Add the corn kernels, cook for 2 minutes, and mix to combine.

6 Strain the pasta and add it to the pan with the mushrooms along with the remaining 3 tablespoons of butter, tossing well to melt the butter. Season with salt and pepper to taste.

7 Distribute the pasta among 4 bowls or large plates. Top each portion with 5 tarragon leaves, grated pecorino Romano, and a large dollop of the smoked ricotta. Grind fresh black pepper over each.

THE VANDERBILT, PROSPECT HEIGHTS

BROOKLYN BREWERY

Building the borough's second golden age of brewing, one lager at a time.

There are now three breweries in Brooklyn—including Kelso in Clinton Hill and Sixpoint Craft Ales in Red Hook, both of which make serious, sought-after suds—but there is only one Brooklyn Brewery, an eighteen-year-old operation that lives in an old ivy-covered warehouse in Williamsburg. Launched by Steve Hindy, a former home brewer and Associated Press foreign correspondent, and Tom Potter, a former banker and neighbor, it's the seventeenth-largest craft brewer in the country by volume, its beers proudly sold in twenty-six states and counting. In fact, Brooklyn Brewery's iconic logo—a cursive green *B* created by Milton Glaser, the famous designer of the "I Heart NY" campaign—is these days not only known in New York City taprooms but a bona fide symbol of America in bars as far away as Brazil. And even if Brooklyn Brewery Lager, Chocolate Stout, and Pennant Ale are now produced in quantity well north of the borough, their world-class, award-winning creator, Garrett Oliver—a brewmaster so respected he was tapped to pen the first-ever *Oxford Companion to Beer*—still brews some of the world's best small-batch, ultra-artisan beers right off one of Brooklyn's hippest main drags.

Like many of America's top craft breweries, one of Brooklyn Brewery's original goals was to make complexly flavored quaffs in a country that—until recently—made very few of them. In the early years, recalls Hindy of his first bottles of Brooklyn Lager, "people would almost spit it out. They would say, 'Oh my God, this is so bitter,' he laughs, "and what they were really saying is, 'Oh my God, this beer has flavor.'" But beyond good beer, Hindy and Potter also wanted to reclaim a bit of the borough's great pre-Prohibition brewing tradition, a period when local brands—Schaefer, Rheingold, Piel's, Edelbrew, William Ulmer, Nassau—were part of the fabric of daily life: you'd see their trucks, you'd drink their beers at ballgames, and likely as not you knew somebody who worked there personally.

"Our original plan was to become a Brooklyn institution, to become important in this community," says Hindy, who learned his local lager history in part from the rarely seen 1976 tome *Breweries of Brooklyn: An Informal History of a Great Industry in a Great City*. (Until he scored a copy as a gift, Hindy had a photocopy made from the public library.) That beery book was written the very year the last of the great Brooklyn breweries—F. & M. Schaefer Brewing Company, once one of the largest in the country—shuttered its long-standing production plant in the neighborhood of Bushwick, where so many beer makers once toiled on a piece of Scholes Street still called Brewer's Row.

At the turn of the last century, in fact, some forty-eight breweries were producing much of the East Coast's beer right in Brooklyn. Many of their brick buildings—nearly all built by Brooklyn's once thriving German immigrant population—still stand tall in Williamsburg and Bushwick. But due to the world wars, the alcohol-free years of Prohibition, the always high costs of doing business in New York City, and perhaps even the loss of New York State's once thriving hop farms to the Midwest, one by one they closed their doors. Once Schaefer left the city in the 1970s, beer wasn't brewed here again until the opening of Brooklyn Brewery in 1993.

And while three breweries is still just a drop in the bucket of a local brewing industry, there's no question that Brooklyn Brewery is helping to pave the way for a new era of local producers, and that Brooklyn, once again, is a city known for its beer.

CRISPY ROAST CHICKEN WITH SAGE

From Gwen Schantz, Brooklyn Grange

Gwen Schantz is a gardener and co-founder of Brooklyn Grange, a multiacre rooftop farm in Long Island City, Queens. Schantz spends the winters gardening in a heated greenhouse on the roof of Roberta's—a pizzeria in Brooklyn that uses Gwen's fine yields in its fantastic salads and pies. Schantz makes this deeply aromatic, essence-of-simplicity chicken often, she says, because sage grows so abundantly at Roberta's that she never runs out of it. Her method of cooking the bird without basting it is a convection-like technique that results in a wonderfully crackly skin. Be sure to invite friends for dinner when you make this—assuming the robustly earthy aroma of the sage doesn't lure your neighbors over first.

Edible Technique

When carving the breast halves, slice them horizontally (against the grain) rather than lengthwise. The result will be firmer, juicier meat that will hold its shape rather than fray.

1 (4–5 LB) WHOLE ORGANIC CHICKEN
1½ TBSP SEA SALT
1 TBSP FRESHLY GROUND BLACK PEPPER
2 TBSP FINELY CHOPPED FRESH SAGE

Serves 4

1 Preheat the oven to 450°F.

2 Pat the skin of the chicken with a clean kitchen cloth or paper towels so that it is completely dry. Place the chicken in a medium-size baking dish or roasting pan.

3 Combine the salt, pepper, and sage in a small dish, and rub the chicken with the mixture so that the whole outside of the bird is well covered with seasoning.

4 Place the chicken in the oven and roast, uncovered, for 1–1½ hours, or until the skin of the bird is golden brown and crispy and the juices run clear or a thermometer inserted into the thickest part of the thigh reads 160–165°F.

5 Remove the chicken and baste it in its pan drippings. Loosely tent it with foil, and let it rest for 10 minutes in the pan. Serve with roast vegetables and potatoes.

BONELESS QUAIL STUFFED WITH FOIE GRAS AND BLACK TRUFFLE MOUSSE WITH BALSAMIC DEMI-GLACE

From Garrett Oliver, brewmaster of the Brooklyn Brewery and author of The Brewmaster's Table

This recipe is quintessential Garrett Oliver, a Renaissance man if there ever was one. As the award-winning brewmaster for Brooklyn Brewery since 1994, he's one of the best minds in beer worldwide, tapped to write the first-ever *Oxford Companion to Beer*. Not for nothing did Carlsberg, the massive Danish brewery, grant Oliver the Semper Ardens award—it's Latin for "always burning"—for beer culture at a dinner in Copenhagen in 2003, at a time when American craft brewers were just starting to be seen as credible. A home brewer and home cook extraordinaire, he grew up in New York City hunting on horseback with his parents, knows plenty about city architecture, design, history, and art, and can hold his own with experts on wine, spirits, and cocktails, too.

Edible Tip

This dish might sound pricey, but the happy secret is that it's actually very affordable. One 6-ounce package of foie gras—enough to stuff all six quail—is around fifteen dollars from D'Artagnan, a specialty meat provider that was the first to import fresh foie gras and other European-style meats in the 1980s and now works with local farms. See *Dartagnan.com*.

1 (6 OZ) PACKAGE FOIE GRAS (BLACK TRUFFLE MOUSSE)

4 PREPARED SEMIBONELESS QUAIL, FIXED WITH A V-SHAPED WIRE INSIDE THE CAVITY

EXTRA-VIRGIN OLIVE OIL

SEA SALT

FRESHLY GROUND BLACK PEPPER

4 CUPS CHICKEN OR DUCK STOCK

3 MEDIUM SHALLOTS, FINELY MINCED

3½ TBSP BUTTER

½ CUP OFF-DRY WHITE WINE

3 TBSP BALSAMIC VINEGAR

2 TSP ALL-PURPOSE FLOUR

Serves 4

1 Put a teaspoon of foie gras mousse on a spoon. Insert the spoon inside the cavity of a quail, pinching the spoonful of mousse with your fingers as you pull the spoon out of the cavity, leaving it inside the cavity. Pin both ends of the cavity shut with toothpicks. Repeat with the remaining quail. Coat each bird with olive oil, and sprinkle with salt and pepper.

2 Heat a large, heavy cast-iron skillet over high heat. Add olive oil to cover, heat it until it simmers, then gently pan sear the birds, breast side down, until browned, about 3 or 4 minutes. Turn the quail over and sear for 2 more minutes, until brown. Remove from skillet and place the quail, breast side up, on foil-covered sheet pans and set aside. (You may have to work in batches.)

3 Preheat the broiler.

4 In a medium saucepan, bring the stock to a boil and cook until it reduces to about a cup. In a small pan, gently sauté the shallots in 1½ tablespoons butter until soft and golden. Deglaze the pan with the wine and turn to a slow simmer. Add the reduced stock and continue simmering. After 5 minutes, add the vinegar. Continue to simmer until about ¾ cup of sauce remains.

5 In a medium saucepan, heat 2 tablespoons butter over medium heat. When a pinch of flour sprinkled into the butter sizzles, whisk in the flour until it forms a thick paste, though not so stiff that it stops bubbling. Continue whisking as the mixture bubbles, being careful not to burn it—about 3 minutes.

6 Add half of the flour-butter mix to the shallot sauce, stir well, and cook for a few minutes to thicken. If it doesn't thicken, add the rest of the flour-butter mixture, stir again, and cook a bit longer. Reduce the heat to warm, and salt to taste, if necessary.

7 Broil the quail for about 3 minutes, until a thermometer inserted in the thickest part of the bird reads 160–165°F. Remove from the oven; if any of the foie gras mousse has extruded from the quail, add it to the shallot sauce and whisk it in well.

8 Place each quail, breast side up, in the center of a warmed plate. Carefully remove the toothpicks, dress each bird with the warm sauce, and serve immediately, preferably with a dark abbey-style ale.

BROOKLYN FLEA

MAINS

69

SUNDAY SHORT RIBS IN CIDER AND TOMATOES

From Michael Hurwitz, director of GrowNYC's Greenmarket program

Michael Hurwitz manages fifty-one farmers' markets in five boroughs and relationships with 230 family farms representing three hundred thousand acres, but he still finds time to visit the stalls in his Carroll Gardens neighborhood—one of eleven weekly markets in Brooklyn—each Sunday. There he stocks up on Cheryl Rogowski's purslane, *shishito* peppers from Lani's Farm, and cheese from Angela Miller's Consider Bardwell Farm. In fact, Hurwitz can tell you exactly where most of the ingredients he uses in this fantastic fall dish were raised: beef from Wilklow Orchards, Samascott Orchards' pear cider, onions from Hector Perez, and celery from Mimomex Farm. For Hurwitz the arrival of September signifies not just the benefits of the harvest but the beginning of football season, which means short ribs marinated in cider and braised for hours. On Sundays he likes to have the masses over to watch his hometown team, the Pittsburgh Steelers, and everyone—from his two-year-old son to his next-door neighbor—knows who they're supposed to root for . . . as well as the provenance of the dinner they'll be served at halftime.

5–6 LB SHORT RIBS
2 TBSP SALT
1 TBSP FRESHLY GROUND BLACK PEPPER
½ LITER CIDER, PREFERABLY PEAR
EXTRA-VIRGIN OLIVE OIL
2 LARGE YELLOW ONIONS, THINLY SLICED
8 SMALL CARROTS, CHOPPED
6 RIBS CELERY, CHOPPED
4 WHOLE VERY LARGE TOMATOES, PREFERABLY HEIRLOOMS, CHOPPED
1⅓ CUPS CHICKEN STOCK
12 OZ OATMEAL STOUT BEER, SUCH AS SAMUEL SMITH
3 SPRIGS ROSEMARY
2 BAY LEAVES
SOFT POLENTA OR MASHED POTATOES, FOR SERVING

Serves 8

1 Cover the short ribs with salt and pepper and place in a large bowl. Pour in the cider and marinate for 3 hours, covered, in the refrigerator.

2 Add enough olive oil to coat the bottom of a large oven-proof roasting pan or Dutch oven with a lid and heat over medium-high until the oil begins to shimmer. Add the ribs and brown well on all sides, about 8 minutes, working in batches.

3 Remove the ribs from the pan, set aside, and wipe out all but a tablespoon or two of the fat. (If using grass-fed beef, there will be much less oil in the pan.) Add the onions and sauté until they begin to soften. Add the carrots, celery, and tomatoes and continue to sauté for several minutes until all are soft.

4 Preheat the oven to 300°F. Add the ribs back to the pan, standing them up on their ends in between the vegetables, and add the stock and beer. The liquid should fill about half the pot, and the ribs should be covered about three-quarters of the way up. If the ribs are very fatty, use less stock and more cider or water.

5 Add the rosemary sprigs and bay leaves, and bring the pot to a low boil. Cover and place in oven. The ribs will be ready to eat after 4 hours, but will be much better if left to braise for 6 hours.

6 Strain the sauce and vegetables through a sieve and return the sauce to the roasting pan to reduce by half. Serve the ribs and sauce over a bowl of soft polenta or mashed potatoes.

FIVE-CHEESE MAC AND CHEESE: WASHED-RIND EDITION

From Patrick Watson, co-owner of Stinky Bklyn, Smith & Vine, the Brooklyn Wine Exchange, and The JakeWalk

When it comes to cheese and wine, Michele Pravda and Patrick Watson are a force in brownstone Brooklyn, running a cheese shop, two wine shops, and a wine and cocktail bar within a few blocks of one another. Lucky indeed are the friends who might get invited over for this over-the-top, five-cheese mac and cheese made with award-winning Pleasant Ridge Reserve from Wisconsin, aged Gruyère from Switzerland, Italian Taleggio, Meadow Creek Dairy "Grayson" from Virginia, and Red Meck from Finger Lakes Farmstead Cheese in upstate New York. Watson credits the origins of the dish to Mom, who made a more plebian version (always with five cheeses—"No cheating") when he was growing up. "We called this beauty the Five-Cheese Pasta," he says, "and still to this day, it puts a smile from ear to ear on all five of us kids, as it did all throughout our childhood."

Edible Technique

To grate a very soft cheese like the Taleggio, says Watson, chill it well, and then "just throw it into the Cuisinart! It might get messy, but don't be afraid." The combination of a few hours in the fridge and a food processor, he adds, makes short work of grating.

1 STICK UNSALTED BUTTER, PLUS EXTRA FOR GREASING
2 LB LARGE MACARONI OR RIGATONI
4 TBSP ALL-PURPOSE FLOUR
4 CUPS WHOLE MILK
3 CLOVES GARLIC, MINCED
SALT
FRESHLY GROUND BLACK PEPPER
2 LB PLEASANT RIDGE RESERVE, RIND REMOVED AND GRATED
1 LB GRUYÈRE, AGED AT LEAST 1 YEAR, RIND REMOVED, AND GRATED
½ LB TALEGGIO, GRATED
½ LB MEADOW CREEK DAIRY GRAYSON, GRATED, OR USE FONTINA OR VACHERIN
½ LB FINGER LAKES FARMSTEAD CHEESE RED MECK, GRATED, OR ANY AGED CHEDDAR, PREFERABLY GRAFTON 4-YEAR
1 TSP CHOLULA HOT SAUCE OR TABASCO
½ CUP PANKO BREAD CRUMBS
½ CUP REGULAR BREAD CRUMBS

Serves 8–10

1 Grease one large baking pan or two small baking pans, making sure to grease the sides. Cook the pasta in boiling, salted water until al dente, drain, and toss in a large bowl with 2 tablespoons butter.

2 In a small saucepan over medium heat, melt the remaining 6 tablespoons butter, and when it begins to foam, add the flour and whisk vigorously for 5 minutes. The mix should turn a reddish brown and smell nutty. Cover and keep warm on lowest possible heat, whisking periodically. (It should not get any darker.)

3 In a heavy, medium-size pot (preferably enamel-coated cast iron) over medium-low heat, warm the milk. Once it begins to steam, add the garlic and stir for 1 minute. Lightly season with salt and pepper to taste. Add the flour-butter mixture to the milk and whisk vigorously for 1 minute to completely blend them, and keep warm.

4 Preheat the oven to 400°F. Mix the cheeses, and set aside 2 cups. Add the rest slowly to the milk, stirring until completely melted (some clumps may remain). Add the hot sauce and stir. Pour the cheese sauce over the cooked noodles and toss. Lightly season with salt and pepper to taste. Pour the mixture into the baking dish or dishes. Sprinkle the reserved 2 cups of cheese on top.

5 Combine the bread crumbs in a bowl and sprinkle them evenly on top of the macaroni and cheese. Bake uncovered for 25 minutes, or just long enough for the bread crumbs to brown. Remove from the oven and let cool for 15 minutes before serving.

THE BROOKLYN FLEA

Where antiques and old records meet pickles and pupusas

Strolling through the Brooklyn Flea on a typical weekend, you can crunch on a sample of The People's Pickles from Rick's Picks, buy an antique magazine rack from Olde Good Things, try on a faux-fur cape from Jellyroll Vintage, and drool over Salvatore Bklyn's homemade whole-milk smoked ricotta.

Still, Eric Demby has a hard time explaining what it is he does. In fact, it's hard to even define the Brooklyn Flea—the wildly successful joint venture he and Jonathan Butler of *Brownstoner. com* launched in April 2008.

"I would say it's a public market," Eric explained. Pause. "It has a little bit of an old-fashioned town square element to it in that it's a meet-up place." Another pause. "It's a country store . . . a tourist destination . . . an entrepreneurial incubator."

Whatever it is, Brooklynites can't seem to get enough. On opening day more than twenty thousand people showed up to browse the hodgepodge of booths in Fort Greene. The next Sunday, ten thousand more joined in the fun and a tradition was born.

From 170 vendors that first day, the event has grown to a twice-weekly two-venue affair in Fort Greene—Saturdays outdoors at a high school, Sundays

inside at the old beautiful beaux arts Williamsburgh Bank Building.

But this isn't just a market. Many of the businesses—DIY start-ups too small to afford commercial spaces—were born in tiny apartment kitchens or unused corners of other businesses. For them, the Flea's cheap booths serve as their sole retail outlet until the business gets big enough, and profitable enough, to set up shop elsewhere.

Take SCRATCHbread's Matthew Tilden. With little more than a dream and a penchant for great bread, Tilden launched his business baking crusty loaves at night when the brick oven at a local pizzeria lay unused. The hours were rough, but he sold enough leavened goods at the Flea to build a following and afford a bakery of his own in Bedford-Stuyvesant.

As unlikely as a market full of antiques, secondhand clothes, and

artisanal food may seem, the combination made sense to Demby and Butler, who used to frequent the famous Chelsea Market in Manhattan in its nineties heyday. As Demby sees it, there's an overlap between people who appreciate an aesthetic of home furnishings with character and people who appreciate handmade food. Plus, "People like to shop and eat," he says, "and if you have both, you have a hit."

An unanticipated by-product is creative collaboration. Nunu Chocolates once shared a table with Crop to Cup Coffee, and soon family-farmed beans made their way into Nunu's espresso truffles. These days, the leftover coffee sacks Crop to Cup uses to import them are repurposed as upholstery for burlap children's chairs at foundation4, and fermented cukes from McClure's Pickles add crunch to the Asian-inspired franks at Asia Dog.

As for those who eat them, Demby knows there's also something special. "It's a really nice cross-section of modern Brooklyn," he says of his young-ish crowd, which is about 50 percent Brooklynites by his estimation, with "a lot of really beautiful people, usually." In fact, Demby knew his market had truly become "a scene" when "people started getting dressed up to go there."

SALSICCE AL VINO E OLIVE NERE
(SAUSAGE WITH WINE AND BLACK OLIVES)

From Arthur Schwartz,
TheFoodMaven.com *and author of
four cookbooks, including*
New York City Food:
An Opinionated History
with Legendary Recipes

Brooklyn native Arthur Schwartz, aka The Food Maven, may be best known as a chronicler of Jewish and New York City foodways—he literally wrote the books on the two subjects—but he's also a bona fide expert on Italian food, running a cooking school on a water buffalo farm near the Amalfi Coast when he isn't home in Park Slope. This dish is collected from his travels there (and its stunning simplicity might reveal its origins: a small town called Caltanisetta, in the center of Sicily), but it's just as connected to his hometown. "I am always joking these days that it's easier to live an Italian life in Brooklyn than in Italy," he tells us. "With the exception of first-quality and absolutely fresh *mozzarella di bufala*, I can get just about every ingredient I need for my Southern Italian cooking in Brooklyn. . . . When I sit in my kitchen I can look at the Montauk Club, a Venetian Gothic building, and best of all, unlike in Italy, after I've waited an hour on line at the post office in Brooklyn, they still have stamps." If you can't easily find fresh Italian sausages, he adds, don't worry: "The red wine and black olive combination has the ability to upgrade even mediocre links and the sausage take on a beautiful, intense mahogany color from the glaze that forms on their surface."

1 LB SWEET ITALIAN PORK
SAUSAGE, PREFERABLY
WITH FENNEL SEED
½ CUP DRY, ROBUST RED WINE

10 TO 12 OIL-CURED BLACK OLIVES

Serves 4

1 Cover the sausage with water in an 8- to 9-inch skillet over high heat. As soon as the water boils, reduce the heat so it gently simmers. Cook the sausage, uncovered, turning them several times once the water evaporates enough to expose the tops of the sausage.

2 When all the water has boiled away, after 15–20 minutes, reduce the heat to very low and, turning the sausage frequently, brown the sausage in the rendered fat in the pan. If you need a bit more fat, prick a couple of the sausages with the point of a knife.

3 When the sausage has browned, add the wine and oil-cured black olives. Increase the heat so the wine simmers. With a wooden spoon, scrape up any glaze left by the sausage on the bottom of the pan.

4 Keep turning the sausage in the wine. Cook the wine until it has reduced to a glaze on the sausage, which will take on a rich mahogany color. This takes only a minute or so. Serve immediately.

Edible Tip

For Southern Italian groceries, Arthur Schwartz heads to the Italian American neighborhood of Bensonhurst. He buys bread at Royal Crown bakery at 6512 Fourteenth Avenue; his sausages and meats from Faicco's, an "old-time" Italian butcher shop at 6511 Eleventh Avenue; and "the best canned peeled tomatoes from San Marzano" and a slew of other goods at D. Coluccio & Sons at 1214 Sixtieth Street. The last, happily, does mail order: *DColuccioandSons.com.*

PEANUTTY NOODLES WITH SEASONAL VEGETABLES

From Jacquie Berger,
director of Just Food

Brooklyn resident Jacquie Berger is the director of Just Food, the nonprofit New York City organization that's largely responsible for connecting dozens of farmers with hundreds of city residents through Community Supported Agriculture buying clubs, also known as CSAs. (They also help citizens start farmers' markets, plan community gardens, raise bees, and build chicken coops.) Needless to say, Berger is often loaded with produce: "I developed a crush on this recipe during the dog days of summer, when it was hot and I had a lot of vegetables around and was hungry," she says. "When summer turned to fall, I discovered the dish was endlessly flexible and adapted well to a wide variety of produce. As the seasons changed, my crush developed, as you always hope they will, into true and lasting love."

Edible Tip

Asian eggplants, which are smaller and far more tender than their larger European counterparts, usually can be cubed and quickly cooked without having to salt and drain them of their water.

12 OZ ORGANIC WHOLE WHEAT
  SPAGHETTI
2 TBSP TOASTED SESAME OIL
1 TBSP PLUS ¼ CUP SOY SAUCE
1 CONTAINER EXTRA-FIRM TOFU,
  WELL DRAINED, PATTED DRY,
  AND CUT INTO LONG STRIPS
  ABOUT ½ INCH THICK
ANY SEASONAL VEGETABLES,
  SUCH AS:
  2 CUPS CUBED ASIAN EGGPLANT
  OR 4 CUPS CHOPPED BOK CHOY
  OR OTHER ASIAN GREENS
  OR 2 CUPS BROCCOLI FLORETS
  OR 2 CUPS COMBINED JULIENNED
  CUCUMBERS, CARROTS, AND/OR
  ZUCCHINI

½ CUP CREAMY, ORGANIC PEANUT
  BUTTER
1 TBSP RICE VINEGAR
SALT
FRESHLY GROUND BLACK PEPPER
HOT SAUCE
1 TBSP CHILE OIL, OR ANOTHER
  HOT SAUCE, IF YOU PREFER

Serves 4

1 Cook noodles in boiling, salted water according to package instructions until tender but still al dente.

2 While the noodles are cooking, set a large sauté pan over medium heat, add 1 tablespoon of the sesame oil and 1 tablespoon of the soy sauce, and sauté the tofu strips until they begin to brown. Add the vegetables to the pan and cook until tender (or wilted, in the case of the greens), 4–5 minutes. Remove from heat, but cover to keep warm.

3 Drain the noodles and run them under cold water for a minute or two. Transfer to a bowl, and toss with the remaining 1 tablespoon sesame oil.

4 Combine the peanut butter, ¼ cup soy sauce, and vinegar and whisk until smooth. Add a little salt, pepper, and hot sauce to taste, and adjust the mix as necessary. Thin the sauce with a bit of hot water, incorporating it into the mixture until the sauce is about the consistency of heavy cream.

5 Pour the sauce over the noodles, coating them completely. Top with the sautéed vegetables and drizzle with chile oil.

CHRISTY HARRISON'S SZECHUAN SPICED BRISKET

*From Christy Harrison,
food writer and master's candidate
in food studies at NYU*

A former editor for *Gourmet.com*, Christy Harrison is one of those cooks adept at knitting together a slew of influences into her own thing. Here the fattiness of traditional brisket is offset by a complex Asian spice blend featuring Szechuan peppercorns, actually the shell of a tiny Asian fruit. Hard to find—try *Penzeys.com*—they provide an amazing blend of floral notes and lip-numbing heat akin to mentholatum. (Using pink peppercorns or chili would still be delicious, but it wouldn't be the same.) It's a mash-up of a *Gourmet* recipe from chef Susan Feniger and a short-rib rub from chef Gray Kunz's book *The Elements of Taste*, as well as an accidental homage to the long-standing New York Jewish custom of Chinese food on Christmas.

Edible Technique

If you don't have a pan large enough to fit four pounds of brisket, do as Harrison does: buy two 2-pound pieces of "second-cut" brisket—a whole brisket is two muscles, and this is the smaller, fattier one—and cook them in two Dutch ovens. Harrison also uses grass-fed beef. If using grain-fed beef, increase the oven temperature to 350°F.

- 1 TBSP ALLSPICE, WHOLE
- 1 TSP WHOLE CLOVES
- 4 TBSP CORIANDER SEED
- 1 BAY LEAF
- 1 TBSP CUMIN SEEDS
- 1 TBSP SZECHUAN PEPPERCORNS
- 1 TBSP BLACK PEPPERCORNS
- 1 TBSP GROUND CINNAMON
- PINCH OF KOSHER SALT
- 4 LB GRASS-FED BEEF BRISKET, KEPT AT ROOM TEMPERATURE FOR 30 MINUTES
- 2 TBSP SUNFLOWER OIL, OR PEANUT OR CANOLA OIL
- 1 SMALL WHITE ONION, CHOPPED
- 2 MEDIUM RED ONIONS, CHOPPED
- 1 BUNCH SMALL CARROTS, ROUGHLY CHOPPED (3 CUPS)
- 5 RIBS CELERY, ROUGHLY CHOPPED
- 6 GARLIC CLOVES, PEELED AND GENTLY CRUSHED
- ½ CUP APPLE CIDER VINEGAR
- 2 CUPS CHICKEN STOCK OR REDUCED-SODIUM CHICKEN BROTH
- 2 (28 OZ) CANS CRUSHED TOMATOES

Serves 8

1 Make the spice rub: Toast the allspice, cloves, coriander seeds, bay leaf, cumin seeds, and Szechuan peppercorns in a dry skillet until fragrant (about 6 minutes). Transfer to a bowl, add the black peppercorns, and grind the mixture in a spice grinder or with a mortar and pestle to a medium-fine powder. Stir in the cinnamon and salt.

2 Season the brisket liberally with the spice rub, working it into the meat on all sides. Reserve any excess spice rub to add to the braising liquid.

3 Preheat the oven to 325°F. Heat the oil in a large Dutch oven with a cover over medium-high heat until shimmering. Add the brisket to the pot and brown on all sides, about 8 minutes total. Transfer to a large platter.

4 Reduce the heat to medium. Add the onions to the pan and cook, stirring, until golden, about 12 minutes. Add the carrots, celery, and garlic and cook until they develop some color, 10–12 minutes, and the surface of the pot begins to dry out slightly. Pour in the vinegar and scrape up all the caramelized bits with a wooden spoon. Add the stock and tomatoes and bring to a simmer.

5 Return the brisket to the pot, nestling it in the braising liquid (the liquid will not cover the meat). Cover and braise in the oven until fork-tender, 3–3 ½ hours. Transfer the meat to a platter, drape loosely with foil, and let rest for 10 minutes.

6 While the meat is resting, strain the cooking liquid through a fine-mesh sieve, and discard the vegetables. Pour the sauce through a fat separator and return to a small saucepan. Bring to a low simmer over medium heat.

7 To serve, slice on the bias, against the grain, and drizzle with the sauce.

CONEY ISLAND BOARDWALK

EGG NOODLES WITH CREAMY RED CABBAGE AND SWEET CORN

From Erin Fairbanks,
cohost of The Farm Report,
Heritage Radio Network

Erin Fairbanks has plenty of experience in farm-to-table eating. She was a former cook at two celebrated Manhattan restaurants, Savoy and Gramercy Tavern, ran a farm camp in upstate New York, and now cohosts *The Farm Report* on Brooklyn's Internet radio station, Heritage Radio Network. This excellent early fall dish, spiked with purple and gold, is also straight from the farmers' market. "Creamy, sweet, salty and sour," says Fairbanks, "I crave this pasta all of the time. It's the type of thing I imagined myself eating as a young girl; me in my candlelit Brooklyn apartment with a steaming bowl of pasta and big glass of wine."

2 TBSP EXTRA-VIRGIN OLIVE OIL
1 LARGE ONION, THINLY SLICED (ABOUT 1 CUP)
3 CLOVES GARLIC, SLICED
1 MEDIUM HEAD RED CABBAGE, CORED AND SLICED INTO STRIPS ½ INCH WIDE
1 TBSP SALT
⅓ CUP RED WINE VINEGAR
¼ CUP SUGAR
1 TBSP UNSALTED BUTTER
1½ CUPS SWEET CORN KERNELS
1 LB WIDE EGG NOODLES
1 CUP CRÈME FRAÎCHE OR SOUR CREAM
FRESHLY GROUND BLACK PEPPER

Serves 4–6

1 Heat the olive oil until shimmering in a large saucepan set over medium heat. Add the onion and garlic, cover the pot, and cook for a few minutes until the onion is a soft tangle but the garlic is not yet golden.

2 Add the cabbage and salt, and cook for 3–4 more minutes, taking care to not let the vegetables brown. Add the vinegar and sugar, cover the pot, reduce to a gentle simmer, and cook for 30–45 minutes, stirring occasionally. Taste the cabbage: it should be tender but not mushy. Adjust the salt, vinegar, and sugar to taste as needed, and set the cabbage aside.

3 In a large skillet, melt the butter and sauté the corn over high heat until it begins to caramelize. Remove from heat and set aside.

4 Cook the egg noodles according to package directions, reserve 1 cup of the pasta water, and drain. In a large bowl, combine the egg noodles, sweet corn, braised red cabbage, and crème fraîche. Thin with pasta water to taste. Ladle into bowls and serve topped with pepper to taste.

SLOW-ROASTED WILD ALASKAN SOCKEYE SALMON

From Christopher Nicolson, assistant winemaker, Red Hook Winery

Christopher Nicolson has two amazing food jobs: first, he's one of the assistant winemakers at Red Hook Winery in south Brooklyn, the borough's first true winery. (They bring in the grapes from the North Fork of Long Island, then crush, blend, ferment, and age on site.) He's also a real fisherman. Though he lives in Brooklyn, his family hails from Alaska, where they set out each summer for wild sockeye and chinook salmon, casting their nets from twenty-foot open skiffs—a ritual he wrote about in an early issue of *Edible Brooklyn*. The family now runs a wild salmon CSA through *RedSalmon.com*, with deliveries of their coveted, deeply flavored flash-frozen fillets—Nicolson says they're nothing like mushy mass-produced fish—to Brooklyn and other cities. Nicolson says to pair this dish, made with the easier-to-source sockeye salmon, with a green salad, boiled rice, and Red Hook Winery's Macari Vineyard chardonnay.

1 (1½ LB) FILLET OF SKIN-ON, WILD ALASKAN SOCKEYE SALMON
1 TSP PEANUT OIL
1 TSP KOSHER SALT
1 TSP SUGAR
1 LEMON, ONE HALF JUICED, THE OTHER HALF SLICED AND RESERVED FOR GARNISH
FRESHLY GROUND BLACK PEPPER
¼ CUP FINELY CHOPPED PARSLEY

Serves 2

1 Preheat the oven to 250°F. Line a sheet pan with parchment paper or aluminum foil. Rinse the fillet under cool water and pat completely dry. Place the fillet on the sheet pan and brush both sides with peanut oil. Season evenly with salt and sugar.

2 Bake for 20 minutes. When pierced with a fork, the fillet should still be slightly translucent, but warmed through.

3 Meanwhile, warm a serving platter. Remove the fish from the oven and place on the warmed platter.

4 Drizzle the lemon juice over the fillet, season with pepper, and garnish with chopped parsley and lemon slices.

EMERGENCY SCALLOPS WITH LEMON PAN SAUCE

From Annaliese Griffin, journalist and editor at BrooklynBased.net

In addition to her teaching duties at the City University of New York Graduate School of Journalism, Annaliese Griffin writes about food and helps run a Brooklyn-centric blog for *The New York Times* and one of Brooklyn's coolest publications, the e-mail newsletter called Brooklyn Based. She's also married to world-class butcher Tom Mylan, who owns The Meat Hook. "Despite the fact that Tom's a butcher," admits Griffin, "we often end up eating fish when we cook at home—meat fatigue, I guess. These scallops take almost no time to prepare, and with a simple green salad you feel pretty healthy, not to mention fancy, eating them for dinner. Scallops are expensive and perishable, so if one of us brings them home, it gives us an excuse to sneak a rare quiet dinner together." Just be sure to shop with care, she adds: "This recipe is very dependent on the quality of the scallops. Try to get the largest, freshest specimens possible."

Edible Technique

Don't skip the extra step of letting the scallops sit after you've patted them dry; it's key to their preparation, and to ensuring a good, golden sear.

1 LB LARGE SEA SCALLOPS, RINSED AND PATTED DRY WITH A CLEAN DISHTOWEL OR PAPER TOWELS
2–3 TBSP EXTRA-VIRGIN OLIVE OIL
SALT
FRESHLY GROUND BLACK PEPPER

JUICE FROM 1 LARGE OR 1½ SMALL LEMONS (ABOUT 2 TBSP)
2 KNOBS OF BUTTER (ABOUT 3 TBSP)

Serves 2

1 Place the scallops on a plate in the refrigerator for about an hour, or until they are completely dry to the touch.

2 Coat the bottom of a heavy pan, preferably cast-iron, with olive oil. Heat over medium-high flame until the oil is shimmering. Do not let the oil smoke.

3 Sprinkle salt and pepper over the top of the scallops so that the mollusks are lightly dusted but not crusted with seasonings. Place the salt-and-pepper side down in the pan and salt and pepper the other side.

4 Sear for 2–3 minutes without moving them, until the underside is a toasty brown color. Remove scallops to two plates, browned side up, leaving any juices in the pan.

5 To make the pan sauce, deglaze the hot pan with lemon juice and reduce the liquid over medium-low heat. Add the butter, whisking until the sauce is thick and well incorporated. Pour the sauce over the scallops.

BROOKLYN BAKED BLUEFISH

*From Ben Sargent, fisherman
and host of the Cooking Channel's*
Hook, Line and Dinner

We've met no man more obsessed with urban seafood than Ben Sargent. He started out making chowder at Hurricane Hopeful, a Brooklyn bar, went on to host a fishing radio show (*Catch It, Cook It, Eat It*) on Heritage Radio Network, made New York City tabloid fame with Dr. Klaw (his rap-style alter ego who delivers what we think are the city's best and butteriest lobster rolls), and now hosts his own show on the Cooking Channel. Sargent also made the cover of *Edible Brooklyn* for his attempts to boost local fishing in the borough through the development of the Brooklyn Urban Anglers Association and a fishing derby with the mission to find "Brooklyn's biggest hooker." Participants often catch bluefish, and when they do, Sargent recommends this recipe from his Massachusetts childhood, which he says is one of the best and easiest ways to cook a blue, sealing in moisture and flavor. If it sounds like a lot of mayonnaise, it is, says Sargent, but that's the point. You can adjust this recipe to bake any size bluefish.

1 WHOLE BLUEFISH (ABOUT 6 LB), CLEANED AND SCALED, SKIN LEFT INTACT

5–6 TBSP MAYONNAISE, PLUS EXTRA IF NEEDED

2 LEMONS, THINLY SLICED

1 LARGE ONION, THINLY SLICED

2 TBSP FRESH DILL, MINCED

1 TBSP OLD BAY

2 TBSP BUTTER, OPTIONAL

Serves 8

1 Preheat the oven to 500°F.

2 Coat the fish with mayonnaise inside and out so that no skin is visible, and place it on a sheet of heavy-duty foil large enough to seal the fish entirely. Layer the fish with lemon slices and onion. Top with dill and dust with Old Bay.

3 Seal the fish in the foil, and place it in a large, heavyweight baking pan. Immediately turn down the oven temperature to 350°F and bake the fish for about 10 minutes per pound.

4 Remove the fish from oven and gently unwrap, being careful of the hot steam. The fish should have some brown crispy parts on the skin when you uncover it. Dot with butter before serving.

Edible Tip

If you're inclined to catch your own bluefish, head out to Brooklyn's Sheepshead Bay neighborhood. There you can hire a captain to take you out for a day of deep-sea fishing, in hopes of netting the big one. Or, if you wait at the docks, you can buy the boats' fresh catch right from the boardwalk.

PAN-SEARED COD WITH SUCCOTASH

From Josh Grinker, chef and co-owner of Stone Park Café in Park Slope

When a pair of childhood friends with the same first name—Josh (Foster) and Josh (Grinker)—opened the Stone Park Café in 2004, they were still two of just a handful of restaurateurs in Brooklyn cooking incredibly flavorful food with a seasonal bent and American sensibilities. Now the restaurant is one of the old guard of the culinary scene in brownstone Brooklyn, crowded nightly and nearly always packed for weekend brunches. That's due to dishes like this one—crispy, succulent cod and bacon and a creamy mix of fresh sweet corn, earthy little new potatoes, asparagus, fava beans, and fennel. It's the kind of dish that shows up only for a few days in very late spring each year, when asparagus and favas and the very first ears of corn are all in season. And it's well worth waiting for.

¼ LB FINGERLING OR NEW POTATOES, DICED
½ LB BACON, CUT INTO ½-INCH BATONS
½ SMALL RED ONION, THINLY SLICED (ABOUT ¾ CUP)
⅓ CUP DICED FENNEL BULB, FRONDS RESERVED, FOR GARNISH
1 TSP FRESH THYME LEAVES
¼ CUP FRESH FAVA BEANS, SHELLED, BLANCHED, AND PEELED
1 CUP FRESH CORN KERNELS
6 SPEARS PENCIL-THIN ASPARAGUS, SLICED INTO 1½-INCH PIECES
⅓ CUP HALF-AND-HALF
1 TBSP CHOPPED PARSLEY
SALT
FRESHLY GROUND BLACK PEPPER
1 TBSP LEMON JUICE
2 TBSP VEGETABLE OIL
6 (6 OZ) COD FILLETS

Serves 6

1 Place the potatoes in a medium saucepan, fill with water to cover by an inch, and bring to a boil over high heat. Reduce the heat just enough to keep the water at a fast simmer and continue to cook the potatoes, uncovered, for 8–10 minutes, or until knife-tender. Drain and set aside.

2 Cook the bacon in a heavy-weight skillet over medium heat until just cooked through. Remove it with a slotted spoon to a bowl, pour off all but 1 tablespoon of bacon grease from the pan, add the onion, and cook until just softened, 2–3 minutes.

3 Add the fennel, thyme, fava beans, and corn, cover, and cook for 2 minutes, or until the fennel is tender. Add the potatoes along with the asparagus, and continue to cook until the asparagus is bright green and warmed through, about 4 minutes.

4 Preheat the oven to 400°F. Add the half-and-half to the pan, increase the heat to medium-high, and simmer until it reduces by half. Add the cooked bacon and parsley and season with salt, pepper, and lemon juice. Remove the succotash from the heat, cover, and keep warm.

5 Place a large, ovenproof, nonstick skillet over medium heat, add the oil, and heat until it shimmers. Pat the cod fillets dry on both sides and season well with salt. Carefully place the fish fillets in the pan and cook without moving them, about 6 minutes. Carefully flip them and place the pan in the oven for another 4 minutes.

6 Ladle the succotash into warm shallow bowls, top with the golden, crispy fish, and garnish with the fennel fronds.

CHAPTER 4

LIGHT SUPPERS AND SOUPS

This is one of our favorite chapters for its remarkable diversity, its dishes drawing inspiration from other countries and continents and from all walks of Brooklyn life. There's a heady coconut and crab soup from the Caribbean; a porky miso broth hailing from the southern tip of Japan; the Sicilian cheese and greens pie reinterpreted by an urban park forager; a cumin and chipotle-spiked parsnip–sweet potato soup perfected by a local farms junkie with an overflowing fridge; and, last but not least, a fried locally caught bluefish sandwich made with housemade tartar sauce and community garden tomatoes on a crusty Italian loaf—the essence of a Brooklyn summer by our own wonderful shore.

"URBAN FORAGER" BITTER GREENS RICOTTA PIE

From Ava Chin, the Urban Forager

In addition to her duties as professor of journalism at the City University of New York, Ava Chin pens a column on urban foraging for *The New York Times* and leads foraging tours of local parks. She chronicles her sidewalk and shrubbery finds, often ending her reports with a recipe. This particular pie—a custardy, deep-dish creation filled with three types of greens and four types of cheese—was inspired by a Corsican friend's family recipe, traditionally made after gathering wild greens on their island homeland. "I became obsessed with trying to re-create this dish using Brooklyn-only foraged plants," says Chin. "The pie's main ingredients change with the seasons—in spring, it can be made with daylily shoots, dandelion leaves, and wild garlic tops." In the fall Chin uses wild dandelions, a wild bitter green called hedge mustard, and the commonly seen triangular-leafed weed called lamb's-quarters—found at farm stands—but nonforagers can substitute cultivated dandelion, mustard greens, and young spinach.

2 SHEETS PREPARED PIE DOUGH, ENOUGH FOR 1 (10-INCH) DEEP-DISH BOTTOM CRUST AND A LATTICE TOP
2 TSP EXTRA-VIRGIN OLIVE OIL
1 MEDIUM ONION, DICED
3 CUPS LAMB'S-QUARTERS OR BABY SPINACH, ROUGHLY CHOPPED
½ TSP SALT
½ TSP FRESHLY GROUND BLACK PEPPER
1 CUP DANDELION GREENS, ROUGHLY CHOPPED

1 CUP MUSTARD GREENS, ROUGHLY CHOPPED
15 OZ FRESH RICOTTA CHEESE
½ CUP PECORINO ROMANO OR PARMESAN
½ CUP FONTINA CHEESE, GRATED, OR ANY GOOD MELTING CHEESE
½ CUP MOZZARELLA, GRATED
3 LARGE EGGS, BEATEN
1 EGG WHITE

Serves 6

1 Press one 10-inch piecrust into an 8-inch springform pan, making sure it goes 1½ inches up the sides of the pan, and set aside.

2 In a large sauté pan, heat 1 teaspoon of olive oil over medium heat. Add onion and cook until soft, about 8 minutes. Remove the onion from the pan and set aside. Wipe the pan and heat the remaining teaspoon of oil over medium heat.

3 Cook the greens in batches: first add the lamb's-quarters and salt and pepper. Sauté about 3 minutes over medium heat. Remove the lamb's-quarters from the pan, keep warm, and add the dandelion greens and mustard greens. Cook another 5 minutes, until all the liquid from the greens evaporates. Add back the lamb's-quarters and cooked onion. Remove from heat and set aside.

4 Preheat the oven to 350°F. In a large bowl, combine the ricotta, Romano, Fontina, mozzarella, and eggs. Add the wild greens and mix well. Spoon the mixture into the prepared pastry crust.

5 Cut the remaining pastry into thin strips and weave it into a lattice pattern over the pie. Mix the egg white with 1 teaspoon water and brush over the pastry crust.

6 Bake until the filling is set in the center and beginning to brown on top, about 40 minutes. Serve warm or at room temperature.

MOZZARELLA: THE WAY OF THE CURDS

From fresh "mozz" to supermarket string cheese, the story of mozzarella begins in Brooklyn.

Decades ago Sal Salzarulo, a fourth-generation cheese maker, received plenty of panicky calls at his Brooklyn store. "I'm having trouble making mozz with that curd I bought from you today. What am I doing wrong?" These days almost no one makes their own fresh mozzarella at home, and as a result Sal oversees an empire producing two hundred thousand pounds a week. His company, Lioni Latticini, is one of the largest producers of fresh mozzarella in the country, selling in forty states to outfits including Whole Foods and Dean & DeLuca. Lioni used to produce everything at one Bensonhurst storefront, but now the retail-only space is retained for sentimental reasons. "We had to move production to a Union, New Jersey, plant because our trucks were getting backed up around the corner," says sales director Mike Virga.

Italians emigrated en masse between 1880 and 1920, including dairymen from southern Italy, where for centuries monks made fresh *mozzarella di bufala*. They soon adapted, making fresh mozzarella from cow's milk, or *fior di latte*. The most enterprising was Neapolitan Giuseppe Pollio, who brought the family cheese-making tradition to Coney Island in 1899, where he sold fresh mozzarella and ricotta. He then opened a store in the neighborhood of Red Hook to supply shops and restaurants, and recognizing the growing demand for "curds" (the fat and protein solids from curdled milk nearly all makers now use rather than starting from fresh milk), bought out competitors and a creamery upstate.

The popularity of pizza in the 1950s spurred cheese makers such as Pollio (by then called Polly-O) to create a low-moisture, meltier mozzarella with a longer shelf life. They stopped handmaking mozzarella in 1947, Lioni followed in 1983—it's now owned by Kraft—but at least a dozen Brooklyn shops sustain the tradition: Caputo's Fine Foods in Carroll Gardens, Landi's Pork Store in Mill Basin, Russo Mozzarella and Pasta in Park Slope, Pizza Mercato in Bay Ridge, Eagle Cheese in Bensonhurst, and just a few blocks away, Pastosa Ravioli, founded by a former Polly-O salesman in 1962.

Today his grandson Anthony Ajello Jr. oversees production—five hundred pounds on a typical Saturday. (Ajello's two Brooklyn uncles own DiPalo Fine Foods in Little Italy, which many consider to make the best fresh mozz in Manhattan.) Yet while neighborhood Italians still manage the registers at Pastosa, a cornucopia of immigrants—particularly Bangladeshis and Mexicans—now expertly make handmade mozzarella. "I give every employee a chance to learn, but you can tell right away who can and can't pick it up," says Russo's owner Jack Cangemi, whose family has been selling mozzarella for ninety-seven years. The technique required might sound simple, but it isn't easy. Massive quantities of curd get sliced and heated in a warm-water bath, then stirred with a metal paddle until they bind together. When they've formed into a mass, you tear off a piece (*mozzare* means "to tear off"), knead it into a ball, and drop it into cool water to stop the cooking.

A lot can go wrong: if the water is too hot, curds disintegrate; too cold and the cheese can't be shaped; over-kneaded, the texture will be like a rock. While Pastosa and Russo pass their knowledge on to employees, other Brooklynites share no such desire. Georgia Teddone, owner of Teddone Latticini in Greenpoint, shaped thirty-five to fifty balls a day until she retired, much to Brooklyn's collective chagrin, at the age of ninety-one in 2010 with no interest in sharing her craft: "I'm taking my secrets," she says, "to the grave."

NEW ZEALAND POTPIE

From Gareth Hughes, owner of Down Under Bakery (DUB) Pies

When New Zealander Gareth Hughes started making Down Under's popular savory meat potpies in Brooklyn, he began with classic Kiwi flavors like the flaky steak and mushroom pies he grew up eating. Now he's expanded the recipes featured at his shop at the southern edge of Prospect Park and sold in bars around the city to include fusion flavors such as Thai Chicken Curry and Chilli Cheese. But this bacon, egg, and cheese breakfast pie might be the big winner, morning or night. "Back in New Zealand, from whence we hail," says Hughes, "a version of this pie was recently voted best pie in the country, and in a savory pie-mad country, that's no small feat." This recipe makes enough for one pie, but with extra dough on hand, it'd be easy to multiply.

1 SHEET PREPARED PIE DOUGH
2–3 STRIPS BACON, CRISPLY COOKED AND BROKEN INTO SMALL PIECES
1 LARGE EGG
SALT
FRESHLY GROUND BLACK PEPPER
2 OZ WHITE NEW YORK OR VERMONT SHARP CHEDDAR, GRATED

1 PREPARED SHEET PUFF PASTRY DOUGH
1 EGG YOLK, FOR BRUSHING THE TOP OF THE DOUGH
1 TSP MILK

Makes 1 (5-inch) potpie

1 Preheat the oven to 350°F. Line a 5-inch potpie tin or deep ramekin with pie dough, and trim the edges. (Reserve excess dough for another use.) Sprinkle the bacon into the pie tin.

2 Break the egg over the bacon, and season with salt and pepper to taste. Top with grated cheese.

3 Moisten piecrust edges with water. Place puff pastry sheet on top and cut to fit, pressing the edges to seal. (Reserve excess pastry for another use.)

4 In a small bowl, whisk the egg yolk with milk. Brush the egg wash on the pie and cut slits in the top for steam to escape. Bake for about 30 minutes, or until pastry is golden brown.

STEAMED BUNS WITH CHINESE SAUSAGE

From Daniel Gritzer, associate food editor at Food & Wine *magazine*

Daniel Gritzer is a native Brooklynite who grew up working in restaurants and published one of his first features in *Edible Brooklyn*—his report on building a brick pizza oven in the backyard of his mother's brownstone. In this recipe he takes on another iconic borough foodstuff: the hotdog. Gritzer gives the frank an ethnic twist courtesy of the yeasty buns and air-cured links called *lap cheong* he buys in Brooklyn's Chinatown, a neighborhood called Sunset Park. "I recently had the idea to make hot dogs using Chinese steamed buns and Chinese sausage," says Gritzer, "sort of a tribute to a classic Brooklyn food and the international community of the borough." The surprisingly snackable result is a little like a cross between the pork buns sold as dim sum and pigs in a blanket.

Edible Tip

Sold in skinny links about 4 inches long and often purchased in pairs, Chinese pork sausages, or *lap cheong*, have a touch of sweetness. They are available at most Chinese supermarkets, but the closest commonly found substitutes are thin sticks of summer sausage or beef jerky sold just about everywhere.

2	ENVELOPES ACTIVE DRY YEAST
2	TBSP PLUS 2 TSP SUGAR
2	CUPS PLUS 6 TBSP ALL-PURPOSE FLOUR
¼	TSP KOSHER SALT
	VEGETABLE OIL, FOR GREASING
½	TSP BAKING POWDER
12	CHINESE PORK SAUSAGES

FOR GARNISH:

HOT CHINESE MUSTARD
SLICED SCALLIONS
CILANTRO
JULIENNED CARROTS
SLICED CUCUMBERS

Makes 12

1 In a small bowl, mix together the yeast, 2 teaspoons sugar, 6 tablespoons flour, and 6 tablespoons warm water to form a wet, sticky dough. Cover with plastic wrap and set aside in a warm place to rise for 30 minutes, or until doubled in size.

2 Transfer the yeast starter to a large mixing bowl and add ⅔ cup warm water, the remaining 2 cups flour and 2 tablespoons sugar, and the salt. Mix until evenly blended. Knead on a very lightly floured counter for 5 minutes, adding no more than a light dusting of flour as necessary to prevent it from sticking, until a smooth, elastic dough forms. Lightly grease the inside of the bowl with vegetable oil. Place the dough in the bowl, cover with plastic wrap, and let rise for 2 hours in a warm place, until doubled in size.

3 Place the dough on a lightly floured surface, sprinkle the baking powder on the surface of the dough, and knead the dough until the baking powder is completely incorporated, about 5 minutes.

4 Cut a piece of parchment paper into twelve 3 x 5-inch rectangles and arrange on a baking sheet. Divide the dough into twelve equal pieces. Roll and shape each piece into a 1 x 4-inch cylinder and place lengthwise atop a parchment rectangle. Lightly grease plastic wrap with vegetable oil and lay it over the dough cylinders, grease side down, to cover. Let rise in a warm place until doubled in size, about 30 minutes.

5 Set up a stackable bamboo vegetable steamer over a saucepan filled one-quarter of the way with water, and bring to a simmer. Carefully transfer each bun, still on its parchment square, to the steamer. Steam the buns, working in batches as necessary, for 15 minutes, or until cooked through.

6 Steam the Chinese sausages until softened, about 15 minutes. (If using a multitiered bamboo steamer, you can steam the sausages and buns at the same time, but be sure that the sausages are on the bottom so that their grease doesn't drip onto the buns.)

7 Split each bun down the center like a hot dog bun, lay a sausage in the center, and garnish with hot Chinese mustard and sliced scallions and a mix of cilantro, julienned carrots, and cucumbers.

SHEEPSHEAD BAY FRIED BLUEFISH WITH TARTAR SAUCE

Annie Hauck-Lawson,
Professor of nutritional sciences
at Brooklyn College

Park Slope native Annie Hauck-Lawson studied Brooklyn's eating patterns for her PhD dissertation. Her subjects included the dedicated fisherfolk found in Sheepshead Bay, where her brother Rob once worked summers as a mate on *The Glory,* a boat in one of the many commercial fleets that dock in the neighborhood. Her family used to rent a beach bungalow nearby, where her mother made hero sandwiches for the lifeguards. "One season while the bluefish were running," says Hauck-Lawson, "we composed the special lunch menu with surfeit from the sea." Those overloaded sandwiches—pan-fried bluefish fillets dredged in a peppery batter and dressed with lemony tartar sauce, shredded lettuce, and tomatoes from the plots she and her brother tended at the nearby Brooklyn Botanic Children's Garden—can now be the highlight of your summer, too.

2 CUPS HELLMAN'S MAYONNAISE
1 SCALLION, FINELY CHOPPED
2 TBSP FLAT PARSLEY LEAVES, CHOPPED
1 TBSP CAPERS, CHOPPED
JUICE FROM ½ LEMON
SALT
FRESHLY GROUND BLACK PEPPER
¾ CUP FLOUR MIXED WITH 1 TSP FRESHLY GROUND BLACK PEPPER
2 EGGS, BEATEN WITH 1 TBSP WATER

1 CUP BREAD CRUMBS, SALTED TO TASTE
VEGETABLE OIL, FOR FRYING
4 (4-INCH) BLUEFISH FILLETS, SKINNED AND PATTED DRY
1 LONG, THIN LOAF ITALIAN BREAD
1 HEAD ICEBERG LETTUCE, SLICED INTO THIN STRIPS
1 RIPE SUMMER TOMATO, THINLY SLICED

Makes 4 sandwiches

1 Make the tartar sauce: mix the mayonnaise, scallion, parsley, capers, and lemon juice together, and add salt and pepper to taste. Refrigerate, covered, until ready to use.

2 Place the flour-pepper mixture, eggs, and bread crumbs on three separate plates. Heat 1 inch of oil in a large, heavyweight skillet (preferably cast-iron) over medium-high heat until it begins to shimmer.

3 Dip the fish fillets into the flour, then the eggs, then the breadcrumbs, and carefully add them to the pan. When golden brown on the bottom, about 2 minutes, flip and fry the other side for about 2 minutes, or until cooked through.

4 Split the bread in half lengthwise and into four sections, and dress the bottoms with the tartar sauce, shredded lettuce, and sliced tomato. Top with the fried fish fillets and more tartar sauce. Replace top halves of bread.

LONG ISLAND CLAMS WITH CHORIZO AND BEER

*From Kara Masi, founder of
Ted and Amy Supper Club*

Kara Masi is one of a handful of bold Brooklynites running secret underground supper clubs from their city apartments, serving up homecooked meals to friends, neighbors, and strangers, and this ideal sop-up-the-sauce clam dish, perfect for entertaining a legal or illegally gathered crowd, was served at one of her recent dinners. Inspired by a trip to Portugal, it takes advantage of the fresh seafood caught off the north shore of Long Island, of which Brooklyn is technically a part. Her clams come from the fishermen who travel to the local farmers' market; the lager is from Kelso of Brooklyn, a craft brewery found just up the street from Masi in Clinton Hill.

3 TBSP OLIVE OIL OR UNSALTED BUTTER

3 CLOVES GARLIC, ROUGHLY CHOPPED

1 MEDIUM YELLOW ONION, CHOPPED

¼ LB SPANISH-STYLE CURED CHORIZO, SLICED ¼-INCH THICK

1 (15 OZ) CAN DICED TOMATOES

6 OZ (½ BOTTLE) BROWN BEER

2 LB LITTLENECK CLAMS OR STEAMERS, SHELLS SCRUBBED

SALT

2 TBSP CHOPPED FLAT-LEAF PARSLEY

CRUSTY FRENCH BREAD OR PORTUGUESE ROLLS

Serves 4

1 Heat the olive oil in a large pot or Dutch oven over medium heat, and sauté the garlic until translucent and fragrant, about 2 minutes. Add the onion and chorizo, and continue to cook until the chorizo begins to brown, about 2 minutes. Add the tomatoes and simmer for about 2 minutes more.

2 Add the beer and the clams, and give the pot a good shake to combine.

3 Cover the pot and bring to a boil for 3–4 minutes. Reduce the heat to medium and simmer until the clams have opened, about 5 minutes.

4 Remove from heat and discard any unopened clams. Taste the cooking liquid and season with salt to taste. Garnish with the parsley, and serve with hunks of bread for sopping up the sauce.

CUCUMBERS WITH RICOTTA, BASIL, AND MINT

*From Andrew Feinberg,
chef and co-owner of Franny's
in Prospect Heights*

Franny's (see profile, opposite) might be known for its ethereal brick-oven pies and tender pastas topped with housemade ragu, but their salads are also stellar. This cool and creamy cucumber salad, featured in an early issue of *Edible Brooklyn*, is especially nice on hot summer nights, when it can practically be dinner on its own. Over the years, they've tinkered with the recipe at the restaurant, removing the chives and using intensely flavored Calabrian chiles, but this recipe still works for us at home.

SALT

2 LB WHOLE CUCUMBERS (PREFERABLY A MIX OF TYPES, SUCH AS KIRBY OR LEMON), SLICED INTO ½-INCH-THICK ROUNDS

1 SMALL BUNCH MINT, LEAVES ONLY

1 SMALL BUNCH BASIL, LEAVES ONLY

1 SMALL BUNCH CHIVES, MINCED

½ CUP FRESH RICOTTA

4 TBSP EXTRA-VIRGIN OLIVE OIL

RED WINE VINEGAR

RED PEPPER FLAKES

FRESHLY GROUND BLACK PEPPER

Serves 4–6

1 Salt the cucumber slices generously in a colander over a bowl and refrigerate for 1 hour. Rinse off the salt and pat them dry.

2 In a medium bowl, toss together the mint, basil and chives. In a separate bowl, whisk together the ricotta and olive oil until it resembles sour cream. Combine with the cucumbers and herbs.

3 Add a few splashes of red wine vinegar, red pepper flakes, and salt and pepper to taste.

FRANNY'S PIZZA

A Brooklyn institution since 2004

In Brooklyn's light-speed contemporary food scene—where the brand new can be forgotten by week two—only a handful of places have remained up-to-the-minute over the years, places such as Diner and Roberta's and Frankies 457, which aren't just packed nightly (and rightfully so) but still capable of a bit of street cred. And Franny's—a little wood-fired, brick-oven pizzeria opened in Prospect Heights by the husband-and-wife team of Andrew Feinberg and Francine Stephens in 2004—is definitely one of those.

It's not as if Franny's is unique in form (pizza in a borough that practically owns the American rights to the genre) or in function (farm to table in a neighborhood where even the corner store stocks local cream). No, here the nightly crowds—families, hipsters, professors, food writers—pressed against the plate-glass window are no longer anxiously awaiting the next big thing, but certifiable deliciousness. This is the kind of intensely satisfying simplicity that most of us find only on vacation. And that's the point: "Find the best products," says chef Feinberg modestly of his Italian culinary inspiration, "and do little to them."

It's a model that works, apparently.

In Franny's ancient lifetime (at least in New York City's culinary years), it has become not just part of Brooklyn's pizza pantheon but a farm-sourced restaurant par excellence, something akin to Chez Panisse rather than beloved Brooklyn pie palaces like Grimaldi's, Totonno's, or Difara's. Culinary cognoscenti far and wide know the place—Blue Hill chef Dan Barber claims it as one of his favorite Brooklyn restaurants—for Stephens's cutting-edge, seasonal

cocktails (best enjoyed, on summer weekend afternoons, on Franny's grapevine-twined back patio); for Feinberg's short menu of housemade charcuterie; and for pizzas, salads, crostini, and a scant handful of pastas whose spare descriptions (Brussels sprouts, *guanciale*, pecorino Romano) veil their power to seriously seduce.

The couple provide even more temptation at Brooklyn Larder, the specialty foods, sandwich, and takeout shop they opened a few doors down on Flatbush Avenue in 2009: Feinberg's

meatballs, bathed in tomato; a hot olive-oil-soaked hoagie stuffed with more of that creamy ricotta and a tangle of warm bitter greens; tubs of gelato in two dozen flavors; plus olive oil sold by the liter, pastas, anchovies, tomatoes, chocolate, charcuterie, and cheese, kept with care in one of Brooklyn's few aging rooms.

If Larder is named for its spirit, Franny's was named for Francine, who met Feinberg when they both worked at the long-standing Manhattan locavore mecca called Savoy. Feinberg was cooking; Stephens was making drinks and going to bartending school. Their first attempt at their own restaurant, a farm-driven place up in the Berkshires, "failed miserably," says Feinberg, so they came back to Brooklyn, working while they searched for both a location and a concept. "We knew it was going to be Italian," says Feinberg. "For me it's just the perfect cuisine. It's not fancy and it goes hand in hand with the whole Greenmarket thing."

When Stephen's brother-in-law suggested a pizzeria, they agree, despite zero experience serving slices. Feinberg admits he continued to tinker for years, but even at first there were ecstatic reviews, and within weeks Franny's was well on its way.

CHEDDAR, PEPPERONI, AND EGG QUESADILLA SANDWICH

*From John Stires,
co-founder of Brooklyn Winery*

Back when they were co-workers at a social media company, John Stires and Brian Leventhal would trek out to Jersey to make wine with their friends. But hauling that much liquid back to the city got tiresome, so the pair decided to bring grape stomping closer to home, opening Brooklyn Winery in Williamsburg, where thirsty Brooklynites with a penchant for DIY can ferment grapes and bottle their own wine. The lovely place—which uses reclaimed wood and materials from brownstones and churches—also serves snacks such as little elegant sandwiches. This addictively eggy cheese and pepperoni snack from Stires—like Williamsburg, a mix of Italy and Latin America—probably isn't considered refined enough to make the wine bar's menu, but it's a fine late-night bite.

¼ **CUP GRATED CHEDDAR CHEESE**
2 **(TACO-SIZE, 6-INCH) FLOUR TORTILLAS (WHITE OR WHOLE WHEAT)**
3 **SLICES LARGE PEPPERONI OR 6–8 SLICES SMALLER PEPPERONI**
3 **LARGE EGGS**

1 **TSP FRESH MARJORAM**
½ **TBSP BUTTER**
TABASCO
SALT
FRESHLY GROUND PEPPER

Makes 1 large sandwich

1 Heat a large stovetop nonstick griddle over medium-high heat.

2 Sprinkle the cheese over one tortilla and top with the second tortilla. Place the tortillas carefully on the griddle and cook on one side until the cheese melts. Flip and cook until the underside is a light golden brown. Place the pepperoni slices down one side of the tortilla and set aside.

3 In a small bowl, beat the eggs together with the fresh marjoram. In a nonstick skillet over medium heat, melt the butter, and when the foam subsides pour in the eggs and scramble until they just come together.

4 Once the eggs are done, remove the pepperoni and cheese tortillas to a plate and top with the eggs.

5 Drizzle with Tabasco and add salt and pepper to taste. Let cool for a couple of minutes, fold it up like a taco, and serve immediately.

JOHN SCHAEFER'S CHILI CON CARNE

From John Schaefer,
host of Soundcheck *and* New Sounds
Live *on WNYC's public radio*

Between his two nationally broadcast radio talk shows, John Schaefer is one of the most influential voices on what's important, interesting, or odd in the world of music. And just as he loves to seek new sounds, he also loves to try new flavors. In the 1980s, long before the burgeoning world of Sunset Park's Mexican tamale and taco trucks hit the big time, Schaefer found a corner store that sold dried Mexican chiles, the crux of this complexly flavored chili. "That bodega is long gone, and various types of dried chiles can now be found readily," he says, "but at the time I thought it was a wonderful thing to be able to make chili con carne that actually used chiles instead of chili powder." He rarely makes it the same way twice, he admits, but this version with whole cinnamon for extra aromatics and unsweetened cocoa and stout beer for extra depth is a keeper. "Don't be put off by the surprising number of chiles," he adds. "This dish is spicy but not ridiculously so."

8 DOZEN DRIED MIXED MEDIUM-HOT MEXICAN CHILES, SUCH AS POBLANO OR ANCHO
2 DRIED CHIPOTLE CHILES
1 FRESH HABAÑERO CHILE
3 LARGE ONIONS, 1 QUARTERED, 2 FINELY CHOPPED
¼ CUP OLIVE OIL
2 LARGE GREEN PEPPERS, FINELY CHOPPED
3 CLOVES GARLIC, FINELY CHOPPED
2 LB GROUND BEEF
1 LB PORK SAUSAGE
1 STICK CINNAMON
1 TBSP GROUND CUMIN
1 TBSP PAPRIKA
1 TBSP OREGANO
1 TSP DRIED BASIL
1 (6 OZ) CAN TOMATO PASTE
1 (28 OZ) CAN CRUSHED OR DICED TOMATOES

3 (15 OZ) CANS BEANS, DRAINED (RED KIDNEY, PINTO, BLACK, OR ANY COMBINATION)
1 (12 OZ) BOTTLE GUINNESS STOUT OR OTHER DARK BEER
2 TBSP UNSWEETENED COCOA POWDER
2 TBSP BROWN SUGAR
1 (16 OZ) BAG FROZEN CORN KERNELS (OPTIONAL)
1 TBSP KOSHER SALT
2 TSP FRESHLY GROUND BLACK PEPPER

FOR SERVING:
MINCED ONION
SOUR CREAM OR YOGURT
GRATED CHEESE

Serves 12

1 Put all the chiles in a medium pot and cover with water. Set over high heat and bring to a boil. Cover, reduce the heat, and simmer for 10 minutes. When the chilies have softened, turn off the heat and let the pot cool. Remove the chiles from the water, reserving the liquid. Cut off the tops of chiles, slit them open, and, using the side of the knife, scrape away the seeds and ribs.

2 Put the chiles in a blender. Add the quartered onion and the reserved chile-cooking liquid, straining out any stray seeds or stems. Blend in batches until smooth, and set aside.

3 In a large stock pot, heat the olive oil. When hot but not smoking, add the chopped onions, green peppers, and garlic and cook until softened.

4 Add the beef and sausage. Cook, breaking up with a wooden spoon, until the meat loses its raw, pink color.

5 Add the cinnamon, cumin, paprika, oregano, and basil, and stir.

6 Add the pureed chiles and onion. Add the tomato paste and stir until mixed into the liquid.

7 Add the canned tomatoes and the beans. If you like your chili thick, mash half a can of beans into a paste before adding to the pot. Add the beer, cocoa powder, and brown sugar. Bring to a low boil.

8 Add the frozen corn, if using. Reduce the heat to a simmer, cover loosely, and let cook for at least an hour, preferably two. Stir occasionally.

9 Add about 1 tablespoon kosher salt and a teaspoon or two of pepper. Stir, turn off the heat, cover loosely again, and let sit for at least 10–15 minutes. Serve with minced onion, sour cream or yogurt, and grated cheese.

TRINIDADIAN *BULJOL*

From Gemma Garcia, beekeeper, East New York Farms!

Hailing from the tiny Caribbean island of Trinidad, Gemma Garcia helps tend the beehives at the massive Brooklyn community garden known as East New York Farms! On Sundays she wakes up early, before mass, to prepare *buljol*, a fresh-tasting, vinaigrette-spiked mix of salty fish, tomatoes, and onion. Garcia likes to eat it with puffy pieces of fried dough known as fry bake but says that this fast fish dish—which is a little like ceviche—is also good with avocados, on crackers, or with pan-fried vegetables. It's made with salted pollack, available in Brooklyn's many West Indian bodegas, but you can easily substitute dried and salted cod (also known as salt cod, or *bacallà* or *bacalao* in Spain, Italy, and Portugal).

12 OZ DRIED SALTED POLLACK OR SALT COD
1 MEDIUM TOMATO, CUT INTO ½-INCH DICE
1 SMALL ONION, CUT INTO ½-INCH DICE
6 GREEN OLIVES, THINLY SLICED
1 SCALLION, THINLY SLICED
3 TBSP EXTRA-VIRGIN OLIVE OIL
FRESHLY GROUND BLACK PEPPER

Serves 4

1 Cover the fish with water in a saucepan and bring to a boil. Cook for 10 minutes, drain, and cover the fish again with cold water. Let sit for a few minutes to cool and release more salt.

2 Remove the fish from the pan and, working over a strainer in a sink, squeeze all the water from the fish with your hands.

3 Place the fish in a large bowl and break it apart with a fork or your fingers. Add the tomatoes, onion, olives, scallion, olive oil, and pepper to taste. Mix well and refrigerate for 5–10 minutes before serving.

EGG IN A NEST

From Emily and Melissa Elsen,
co-owners of Four & Twenty
Blackbirds in Gowanus

Emily and Melissa Elsen grew up in South Dakota, working for the restaurant their mother, Mary, ran with her sisters. But their grandmother Liz's job was to make the pies—strawberry-rhubarb, chocolate cream, pumpkin, and apple—and it was her baking prowess that made the strongest impression. When Emily and Melissa ended up living in Brooklyn, the itch to bake—and to open up the family's second sister-run operation—blossomed. At first they sold their butter-crusted, beautiful pies—salted caramel apple, thyme-scented farmer cheese, rhubarb with grapefruit bitters often made with fruit their father sends from his yard in South Dakota—out of their apartment. But when a lovely little spot opened up near the Brooklyn art gallery that Emily ran, they jumped at the chance to open a real bakery. Their pies are the reason *Food & Wine* magazine and Martha Stewart have raved, but what also keeps regulars returning is housemade sodas and savories such as fresh herb quiches, and this cheesy egg custard with a buttermilk biscuit center. The sisters gently break the dough apart just a tiny bit with their fingers, so that when the biscuit bakes, it spreads more fully across the ramekin, making for a prettier presentation. It's like a bacon-egg biscuit in reverse and will blow minds at any brunch party. The entire recipe can easily be halved if you're treating just yourself, or freeze half of the biscuit recipe to make more later.

1½ CUPS UNBLEACHED
    ALL-PURPOSE FLOUR, PLUS
    ADDITIONAL IF NECESSARY
½ CUP WHOLE WHEAT FLOUR
2 TSP BAKING POWDER
½ TSP BAKING SODA
1 TSP SUGAR
½ TSP SALT
1–2 TBSP FRESH CHOPPED HERBS
    (SUCH AS ROSEMARY, THYME,
    OR CHIVES)

1 STICK COLD UNSALTED BUTTER,
    CUT INTO ¼-INCH PIECES
¾ CUP BUTTERMILK, PLUS
    ADDITIONAL IF NECESSARY
½ LB SHARP CHEDDAR CHEESE,
    CUT INTO ¼-INCH CUBES
20 LARGE EGGS
1 CUP HALF-AND-HALF

Serves 12

1 Preheat the oven to 425°F.

2 Prepare dough for buttermilk biscuits: in a large bowl, whisk together the flours, baking powder, baking soda, sugar, salt, and herbs.

3 Cut the butter into the flour using a pastry blender or your fingertips, working quickly, until it resembles a coarse meal. Pour in the buttermilk and stir with a spatula until the dough comes together in a ball. If the dough seems dry, add an extra tablespoon or two of buttermilk.

4 Turn the dough out onto a floured work surface. Quickly bring the dough together with your hands and roll into a log, adding flour if the dough is still sticky. Divide the dough into 12 equal pieces.

5 Butter twelve 4-inch ramekins measuring 4 inches wide by 2½ inches deep and arrange on a baking sheet. (You could also use extra-large muffin tins.) Divide the Cheddar cubes evenly among the ramekins, sprinkling them across the bottom of each.

6 Whisk together the eggs and the half-and-half until well combined; pour evenly among the ramekins over the cheese to about halfway up the sides of the dish.

7 Place one piece of biscuit dough in the egg mixture in the center of each ramekin, turning the dough to coat it fully with the egg mixture.

8 Bake in the center of the oven until the biscuits are golden brown and done in the center, 18–22 minutes. They will puff up very high and possibly bubble over. Let cool for 10–15 minutes before serving.

CONCH CHOWDER

Jacques Gautier, chef/owner of Palo Santo restaurant in Park Slope

This wonderfully flavored yet surprisingly simple seafood stew—both creamy and spicy, it's inspired by the Caribbean and perfect for cool evenings—was featured in a profile of Palo Santo, a Pan-Latin neighborhood restaurant in Park Slope. Its owner, chef Jacques Gautier, spent his childhood learning about food from his Haitian, Cuban, Dominican, and Puerto Rican relatives, later expanding his repertoire to include Mexican influences—such as the homemade tortillas on page 30—after working side by side with his kitchen staff, most of whom are native to the country. The restaurant is on the ground floor of the brownstone where he lives—both are a beautiful mix of found and forged wood, stone, glass, and modern copper metalwork—and farms in warm weather, raising much of the restaurant's tomatoes, chiles, and incredibly flavorful and diverse salad greens (more than a dozen kinds, from red leaf and arugula to mizuna and lamb's-quarters) in lightweight containers on his roof. Gautier recommends you serve this dish with bowls of steaming white rice.

2 TBSP EXTRA-VIRGIN OLIVE OIL
2 SHALLOTS, MINCED
2 CLOVES GARLIC, MINCED
1 SCOTCH BONNET PEPPER, SEEDED AND MINCED, OR USE HABANERO PEPPERS
1½-INCH PIECE FRESH GINGER, PEELED AND MINCED
¼ LB CONCH MEAT, TAKEN FROM THE SHELL AND CHOPPED, OR USE CHOPPED SQUID, CRAB, OR LOBSTER MEAT
LEAVES FROM 4–5 SPRIGS PARSLEY, CHOPPED
2 LIME LEAVES OR 2 BAY LEAVES
1 TSP GROUND CUMIN
1 TSP GROUND CORIANDER
1 TSP FRESHLY GROUND BLACK PEPPER
2 OZ RUM (DARK OR LIGHT)
1 QT FISH OR SHELLFISH STOCK
½ LB YUCCA ROOT (ALSO CALLED CASSAVA OR MANIOC), PEELED AND DICED, OR SUBSTITUTE POTATOES
1 (15 OZ) CAN COCONUT MILK
SALT

Serves 4

1 Heat the oil in a small stock pot over medium heat, and sauté the shallots, garlic, Scotch bonnet pepper, and ginger for 10 minutes, or until softened. Add the conch and sauté until it just begins to brown, about 7 minutes.

2 Add the parsley, lime leaves, and spices, and mix well. Deglaze the pan with rum, letting the alcohol reduce slightly. Add the stock, bring to a boil, reduce the heat, and simmer for 1 hour, partially covered.

3 Add the yucca and simmer until cooked through, about 10 minutes.

4 Add the coconut milk, give it a stir, and let simmer for 5 minutes, uncovered. Season to taste with salt.

Edible Tip

Brooklyn is home to the world's second-largest Caribbean population, and, as a result, three of the ingredients this recipe calls for—the hot, floral peppers called Scotch bonnets; the meat of the giant ocean mollusk known as the conch; and the stubby brown tubers called yucca or cassava, which must be cooked to be safely eaten—are easy to find in the borough. Elsewhere, you can easily substitute habanero chiles; squid, crab, or lobster meat; and potatoes, respectively.

ROASTED PARSNIP AND SWEET POTATO SOUP WITH FRESH APPLE SALSA AND PARSNIP CRUMBS

From Karol Lu, cook-off champion

Like other American cities, Brooklyn is in the middle of a modern homemaking boom, complete with pickling parties, potluck dinners, and plenty of cook-offs from apple pie and chili to hot dogs, barbecue, cupcakes, and casseroles. With more than thirty such competitions under her belt since 2006, Karol Lu is a competitive cooking veteran, and winner of many titles for multifaceted dishes like this one. A surprisingly addictive blend of apples and root vegetables, it was named both Audience Favorite and Second Place Judge's Choice at a contest called Souperama by a panel that included *Edible Brooklyn* editor in chief, Gabrielle Langholtz. It's pretty much a poster child for how great winter produce can be, which is not surprising, as it was inspired by what arrived with Lu's weekly CSA farm share box in early March.

2 MEDIUM APPLES, PEELED AND CORED, 1 GRATED AND 1 FINELY CHOPPED
1 SMALL RED ONION, FINELY MINCED
½ SMALL BUNCH CILANTRO, STEMMED AND FINELY CHOPPED
JUICE FROM 1 FRESH LIME
SALT
CAYENNE PEPPER
VEGETABLE OIL, FOR FRYING
4 PARSNIPS, PEELED, 1 FINELY DICED AND 3 CUT INTO MEDIUM DICE
SMOKED HOT PAPRIKA

2 SWEET POTATOES, PEELED AND DICED
2 TBSP EXTRA-VIRGIN OLIVE OIL
4 TBSP UNSALTED BUTTER
3 CLOVES GARLIC, CHOPPED
1 LARGE YELLOW ONION, CHOPPED
1 CHIPOTLE CHILE IN ADOBO SAUCE, CHOPPED
1 TBSP ADOBO SAUCE
2 TSP GROUND CUMIN
⅛ TSP GROUND CINNAMON
4 CUPS VEGETABLE STOCK (UP TO 6 CUPS IF OMITTING CREAM)
½ CUP HEAVY CREAM (OPTIONAL)

Serves 4

1 Preheat the oven to 400°F.

2 To make the salsa, mix the grated apple, red onion, and cilantro in a bowl. Add the lime juice, salt, and cayenne pepper to taste, and set aside.

3 To make the parsnip crumbs, coat a heavy-bottomed pot with an inch of oil and heat over medium until shimmering. Working in batches, fry the finely diced parsnip until lightly golden, about 3–5 minutes, and using a slotted spoon, lift out onto a paper towel. Season with salt and paprika to taste, and set aside.

4 In a medium bowl, combine the rest of the parsnips together with the sweet potatoes and olive oil, and season with salt and pepper. Spread on a baking sheet in a single layer and roast in the oven for about 45 minutes, until soft. Set aside.

5 Melt the butter in a medium soup pot over medium heat, and sauté the garlic and yellow onion until soft. Add the chopped apple, roasted parsnips and sweet potatoes, chipotle chile, adobo sauce, cumin, cinnamon, and salt and pepper to taste. Stir in 4 cups vegetable stock and let simmer for at least 30 minutes.

6 Let cool briefly, and carefully puree soup in batches in a blender until very smooth. Mix in heavy cream, if using, and adjust seasonings to taste, adding more stock if needed to thin the soup out. (You could also omit the cream and add 1–2 cups more stock, to taste, instead.)

7 Serve the soup in individual bowls topped with salsa and a sprinkling of parsnip crumbs.

MISO SOUP WITH BERKSHIRE PORK AND
SEASONAL VEGETABLES (*TONJIRU*)

*From Akiko Nishimura,
founder of Akiko's Cookie*

A native of Japan, Akiko Nishimura is a Brooklyn pastry chef known for her incredibly elegant whole-wheat cookies in two flavors (green tea, almond); the Japanese spirit called *shochu*; and chocolate (macadamia nut and vanilla bean). At home, she also perfects simple yet savory dishes—like this outstanding traditional pork stew. The dish, and the Kurobuta, or black-skinned pig, it's traditionally made with, are both from Kagoshima, at the southern tip of Japan. "This is Kagoshima's ultimate comfort soup," says Nishimura of her *tonjiru*, which in the States can be made with Berkshire breeds of pork. Nishimura recommends you eat it with a bowl of Japanese rice: "It makes a complete meal," she says, "that immediately makes me feel at home and energized."

1 LB BONELESS PORK LOIN, PREFERABLY BERKSHIRE, CUT INTO PIECES ¼ THICK AND 3 INCHES WIDE

1 TSP SEA SALT

¼ CUP SAKE OR *SHOCHU*

1 SMALL BURDOCK ROOT, SCRUBBED AND CUT INTO ½-INCH PIECES

2 MEDIUM CARROTS, PEELED AND CUT INTO 1-INCH PIECES

1 MEDIUM DAIKON RADISH, PEELED AND CUT INTO PIECES ¼ INCH THICK AND 2 INCHES WIDE

1 LB JAPANESE SWEET POTATO OR YAMS, PEELED AND CUT INTO 2½- x 1½-INCH PIECES

½ CUP MISO PASTE, PLUS ADDITIONAL, TO TASTE (PREFERABLY ORGANIC, COUNTRY-STYLE WHITE MISO)

1 BUNCH SCALLIONS, MINCED, FOR GARNISH

GRATED FRESH GINGER, FOR GARNISH

Serves 6

1 Massage the pork with the sea salt, toss with the sake, and set aside.

2 Bring 6 cups of water to a boil in a large pot set over medium-high heat, add the pork and sake, and cook at a rolling boil for 4 minutes. Skim the surface of the soup with a wire strainer to remove excess oil and scum.

3 Add the vegetables and cook until tender, about 8 minutes more. Turn off the heat. Add ½ cup of miso paste and stir with a spoon or chopsticks to blend well. Add more miso to taste.

4 Serve in warm bowls, topped with minced scallion and ginger.

CHAPTER 5

DRINKS AND DESSERTS

In a borough that's home to a cocktail culture

par excellence, there's no reason to save a good drink for the finale of your meal—or dessert, for that matter. Better still, the concoctions in this chapter span our community. There's the 1914 drink called the Brooklyn, plus a new White Manhattan made with a corn whiskey produced right in the borough. There's classic tiramisu, a tea-scented panna cotta with blueberry basil, and three kinds of ice cream—spicebush, Concord grape, and honeymint. And, of course, espresso truffles made by one of the borough's artisan chocolatiers, with beans sourced from a local company. Be careful: like Brooklyn, they're addictive.

APPLE VODKA AND APPLE ROSEMARY COCKTAIL

*From Amelia Coulter,
founder of Sugarbuilt*

Amelia Coulter isn't exactly an ordinary sugar-cookie baker. Long before she breaks out her pastry bags, this trained sculptor sketches out the intricate designs she will later render in royal icing. From anatomical hearts and Brooklyn stoopside ironwork to Cuisinarts, fennel bulbs, and lingerie, Coulter's designs gather inspiration from the Brooklyn patterns and architecture around her, leaving other desserts to crumble into (cookie) dust. When she isn't making fancy sweets, Coulter also enjoys producing fancy cocktails, like this impressive drink featuring vodka infused with supremely crisp and juicy Honeycrisp apples—"what every apple wishes it were," says Coulter—and rosemary-flavored syrup. Start this recipe 3 weeks in advance, for maximum flavor.

3 LARGE HONEYCRISP APPLES, 2 CORED AND CUT INTO ½-INCH CHUNKS
1 750-MILLILITER BOTTLE VODKA
1 CUP SUGAR
LEAVES FROM 6 ROSEMARY SPRIGS, PLUS EXTRA SPRIGS FOR GARNISH
½ OZ CALVADOS APPLE BRANDY
2 TSP LEMON JUICE

*Makes 1 bottle of Apple Vodka
(and 1 Apple Rosemary Cocktail)*

1 At least 3 weeks in advance of serving, make the vodka: place the apple chunks into large mason jars and cover completely with vodka, reserving the bottle for later use. Seal the jars and store in a dark place for at least 3 weeks, turning them every day or two. Discard the apple pieces and strain the liquid through a cheesecloth-lined sieve into a quart container with a lid, or through a funnel and back into the reserved vodka bottle.

2 When you're ready to make the drink, prepare the syrup at least several hours in advance or the night before: heat 2 cups water with the sugar and rosemary in a large saucepan over medium heat until the sugar is completely dissolved and the rosemary has lost its green color. When done, the syrup should be slightly amber and taste like sweet rosemary. Discard the rosemary. Cool the syrup, and set aside in its saucepan.

3 Preheat the oven to 200°F. Using a mandoline or other handheld slicer, slice 1 whole apple—stems and seeds included—to about ⅛-inch-thick pieces. Dip the apple slices into the rosemary syrup and lay flat on a silicone- or waxed-paper-covered baking sheet. Bake until completely dry and golden, at least 1 hour. (They might still feel soft once they're dry, but if you remove them from the oven they should immediately become brittle.)

4 When the apple crisps are totally cool, gently bend the baking mat away from the slices and lift them off, letting them rest on a cool, flat surface until you make the cocktail.

5 To make the cocktail, fill a shaker with ice. Add 2 ounces homemade apple vodka, the Calvados apple brandy, the lemon juice, and 2 teaspoons homemade rosemary syrup. Cover, shake well, and strain into a martini glass. Float an apple chip and a rosemary sprig on the surface of the cocktail.

THE BROOKLYN

Despite many attempts over the past century, our namesake cocktail is still up for grabs.

The first we hear of a Brooklyn Cocktail is 1910, when the Louisville *Star-Journal* wrote that such a thing was making the rounds in Manhattan's bars and wondered aloud if it was a soporific. (Brooklyn did not enjoy its current reputation for cultural dynamism.) It was only a matter of time: Manhattan had had its own cocktail since around 1880. But when in 1907 everybody started drinking something known as the Bronx Cocktail, Brooklyn had to act.

And, it turns out, act again—and again and again. . . . This first Brooklyn Cocktail, you see, did not take. Whether that's because its inventor was Wack (literally—Henry Wellington Wack), or because he was a lawyer rather than a bartender, or because he lived in Long Beach, not Brooklyn, or finally because his drink was merely a Perfect Martini with a dollop of raspberry syrup, it sank almost without a trace. The same goes for the second Brooklyn Cocktail, also from 1910. Invented by a Cincinnati German who at least had the good grace to work in the borough, it, too, failed. The fact that it combined absinthe, hard cider, and ginger ale could not have helped its fate.

But there was still a perceived need. The next to try to meet it was likely the Waldorf-Astoria, then on the site now occupied by the Empire State Building. The drink—it appears in a 1914 booklet (*Drinks*, by Jacques Straub) drawing heavily on that hotel's bar book—is a thoroughly professional effort combining rye whiskey, dry vermouth, maraschino liqueur, and the delightful French aperitif Amer Picon.

Yet it, too, barely registered. Even though it made it into the classic *Savoy Cocktail Book*, you never hear of anybody actually drinking the thing, at least not until the current revival. It went unmentioned in December 1934, when after a long search *The Brooklyn Eagle* crowned a concoction by Brad Dewey of Gage & Tollner's as "THE Brooklyn Cocktail." (The formula? Gin, grapefruit juice, and grenadine—or was it Jamaican rum, lime juice, and grenadine? The newspaper claimed the former, Dewey the latter.) Gage & Tollner's might have been Brooklyn's oldest and most beloved restaurant at the time, but not even that could prevent Dewey's creation from falling victim to the fate of its predecessors.

The Eagle found several, for whatever good it did, because by 1945 all were forgotten when the Bronx borough president pointedly asked why Brooklyn had no drink of its own.

Earlier Brooklyns were considered and found wanting. Old-timers from the dusty precincts of the Brooklyn Club claimed one from 1883: unfortunately, said drink was simply a Manhattan made with Jamaican rum, a combination so infelicitous that it simply would not do. Cocktails were created by the score. Result? Seven years later, the industrial designer Norman Bel Geddes asked in the *Eagle* why "there [couldn't] be a Brooklyn cocktail in Dodgertown?" It would have to be garnished, he mused, "with a razzberry."

The sixties and seventies had little interest, but the modern cocktail revival brought serious mixologists back to Brooklyn, and with them love for the 1914 recipe from the Waldorf-Astoria: a solid B+ if not A– classic, which easily puts it on par with the Bronx. (The Manhattan, however, is a straight A+.) New mixologists have also generated many a serious attempt at a new Brooklyn Cocktail, yet try ordering one anywhere but the bar that first made it. If there's one thing the story of the Brooklyn Cocktail teaches us, it's that that our gap doesn't want to be filled. Let Manhattan be a cocktail; let the Bronx be a lesser one, doomed to live in the shadow of the first. Brooklyn don't play like that.

BROOKLYN COCKTAIL
1883

1½ OZ SMITH & CROSS
   JAMAICAN RUM
1½ OZ MARTINI & ROSSI
   RED VERMOUTH
2 DASHES ANGOSTURA BITTERS
1 THIN STRIP LEMON PEEL

Stir the rum, vermouth, and
bitters well with ice. Strain into
a chilled cocktail glass and twist
lemon peel over the top.

BROOKLYN COCKTAIL
1910

1½ OZ TANQUERAY
   LONDON DRY GIN
½ OZ NOILLY PRAT
   DRY VERMOUTH
½ OZ MARTINI & ROSSI
   SWEET VERMOUTH
1–1½ TSP RASPBERRY SYRUP

Shake the gin, vermouths, and
syrup vigorously with ice. Strain
into a chilled cocktail glass.

BROOKLYN COCKTAIL
1914

1½ OZ RITTENHOUSE
   BONDED RYE WHISKEY
1½ OZ NOILLY PRAT
   DRY VERMOUTH
½ TSP LUXARDO
   MARASCHINO LIQUEUR
½ TSP AMER PICON OR ½ TSP
   AMARO CIOCIARO AND 1 DASH
   REGAN'S ORANGE BITTERS NO. 6
1 THIN STRIP LEMON PEEL

Stir the whiskey, vermouth,
maraschino liqueur, and Amer
Picon well with cracked ice. Strain
into a chilled cocktail glass and
twist lemon peel over the top.

BROOKLYN COCKTAIL
1934

2 OZ SMITH & CROSS JAMAICAN
   RUM OR PLYMOUTH GIN
1 OZ FRESH-SQUEEZED LIME JUICE
   OR WHITE GRAPEFRUIT JUICE
2 TSP GRENADINE,
   PLUS MORE, TO TASTE
1 MARASCHINO CHERRY

Shake the rum, lime juice, and
grenadine well with ice. Strain
into a chilled cocktail glass and
garnish with a maraschino cherry.

RECIPES BY DAVID WONDRICH

BROOKLYN COCKTAIL
1944

2 OZ RITTENHOUSE BONDED
   RYE WHISKEY
SCANT ½ OZ MARIE BRIZARD
   APRICOT BRANDY
½ OZ FRESH-SQUEEZED
   LEMON JUICE
1 MARASCHINO CHERRY

Shake the whiskey, brandy, and
lemon juice vigorously with ice.
Strain into a chilled cocktail glass
and garnish with a maraschino
cherry.

BROOKLYN COCKTAIL
1945

½ TSP SUPERFINE SUGAR
1 TSP SELTZER
2 DASHES REGAN'S ORANGE
   BITTERS NO. 6
2 OZ FAMOUS GROUSE BLENDED
   SCOTCH WHISKEY
1 GREEN MARASCHINO CHERRY
1 THIN STRIP LEMON PEEL

Combine the sugar, seltzer, and
bitters in an old-fashioned glass.
Add the whiskey and 2 large ice
cubes, and stir. Add a green maraschino cherry, and twist lemon peel
over the top.

THE GENTLEMAN'S COMPANION

From Kathryn Weatherup, owner of Weather Up in Prospect Heights

Decked-out bars dedicated to the rejuvenated art of drink making have blossomed throughout Brooklyn, and Kathryn Weatherup's eponymous spot is one of the most stunningly beautiful. Opened in 2008, it's all long copper-top counters, vaulted, white-tiled ceilings, and mahogany wood, and a place where Raymond Chandler, had he been an East Coaster, would have fit right in. This lovely drink is her take on one from Chandler's era. Originally called Remember the Maine, after the huge ill-fated military vessel, it was created during the Cuban Revolution and recorded in Charles Baker Junior's 1939 book *The Gentleman's Companion: Being an Exotic Drinking Book or Around the World with Jigger, Beaker and Flask.* As Weatherup reminds us, Baker asks us to "stir briskly in clock-wise fashion."

2 OZ RYE WHISKEY
¾ OZ ANTICA CARPANO FORMULA SWEET VERMOUTH
¼ OZ CHERRY HEERING LIQUEUR
1 DASH ABSINTHE

ICE
1 MARASCHINO CHERRY

Makes 1 drink

1 Chill a drink-mixing glass and a stemmed cocktail glass.

2 Put the whiskey, vermouth, cherry liqueur, and absinthe into the mixing glass, top with the ice, and stir briskly until chilled.

3 Strain into the chilled cocktail glass, and garnish with a cherry.

Edible Idea

Bartenders recommend that you buy true maraschino cherries, or sour cherries preserved in maraschino liqueur, made from a Croatian cherry called Marasca. If you can't find those, look for Dell's: since 1949, the Brooklyn family business has produced the more common flavored preserved fruits dyed a bright red.

KOMBUCHA MUDDLED MINT JULEP

From Eric "Kombuchman" Childs, co-owner of Kombucha Brooklyn

Kombucha is now so popular in Brooklyn that devotees can buy their daily bottles in ordinary convenience stores. Eric Childs was one of the first to market his version—and he knows what works best with its strangely addictive, astringent properties. In this case, a muddled mix of mint, honey, bourbon, and kombucha make for a surprisingly refreshing (and healthy!) julep.

1 LARGE SPRIG FRESH MINT
2 OZ BOURBON
4 OZ KOMBUCHA
1 TSP RAW HONEY DISSOLVED IN 1 TBSP WARM WATER
3 ICE CUBES

1 STRIP ORANGE PEEL SPEARED WITH 1 (4-INCH) STALK LEMONGRASS, FOR GARNISH

Makes 1 drink

1 Muddle the mint in the bottom of a whiskey glass, and top with ice.

2 In a cocktail shaker, gently shake the whiskey, kombucha, dissolved honey, and ice. Strain into the glass. Garnish with orange peel and lemongrass.

CHRISTMAS IN A CUP

From Alie Shaper, owner/winemaker at Brooklyn Oenology

Using grapes grown and fermented in the very nearby North Fork of Long Island—the peninsula of land that Brooklyn shares with its eastern neighbor—Alie Shaper makes wines under the Brooklyn Oenology label and runs a wine-tasting room in Williamsburg. This spiced quaff is the kind that makes you keep your fingers crossed in February for more snowy days. "It is my personally perfected fresh recipe," says Shaper, "which I developed after I was first taught how to make spiced wine during my first wine job ten years ago. It is truly a beverage to warm anyone's stomach and limbs in the dead of winter." Shaper uses Brooklyn Oenology Social Club Red, primarily a mix of Merlot, Cabernet Franc, and Cabernet Sauvignon, but you can substitute your favorite Bordeaux-style blend. Leftovers are also fine to reheat with a touch of water, and be sure to hang on to your spice packet, says Shaper: it's good for up to three batches.

12 WHOLE ALLSPICE BERRIES
12 WHOLE CLOVES
1 WHOLE NUTMEG SEED
15 LARGE CINNAMON STICKS
¼ CUP DRIED LEMON AND/ OR ORANGE ZEST, ROUGHLY CHOPPED
2 BOTTLES RED WINE, PREFERABLY CABERNET FRANC OR CABERNET SAUVIGNON
¼–⅓ CUP DARK BROWN SUGAR
INEXPENSIVE BRANDY OR RUM (OPTIONAL)

SPECIAL EQUIPMENT: CHEESECLOTH

Serves 8–10

1 Crush the allspice, cloves, nutmeg, and 5 of the cinnamon sticks into smallish pieces in a mortar and pestle or with a rolling pin and mix with the dried citrus peel. Bundle the mixture up in a small piece of cheesecloth and tie it at the top, making a sachet.

2 Pour the wine into a medium pot over medium-low heat. Heat slowly until the wine begins to steam, but do not let the wine come to a boil. Turn off the heat and add brown sugar to taste. Stir to dissolve the sugar completely, and add the bag of spices. Let rest for 30 minutes to 1 hour, stirring occasionally.

3 Remove the spices when the mixture is flavored to your taste. Warm the mixture and serve as is, garnished with a cinnamon stick, or pour an ounce of brandy or rum into the bottom of a cup or mug, and then ladle in the spiced wine to fill the glass.

WHITE MANHATTAN

*From Kings County Distillery
and Marlow & Sons restaurant,
Williamsburg*

Forget Kentucky: Brooklyn's Williamsburg neighborhood is now blessed with three micro-distilleries, thanks to new laws that allow those using local grains to score a license to make hard liquor. The first to produce Brooklyn booze was Kings County Distillery, whose initial offering—of the high-proof corn-based spirit called Kings County Moonshine, available nationally from *AstorWines.com*—is so small that their plain glass bottles can come with typewritten labels. This version of the classic Manhattan cocktail, says co-owner David Haskell, was developed just for the spirit by the barkeeps at the restaurant called Marlow & Sons. As he says, "It's simple and fantastic."

2½ OZ KINGS COUNTY MOONSHINE, OR USE ANOTHER CORN WHISKEY

½ OZ DOLIN VERMOUTH DE CHAMBERY BLANC, OR USE ANOTHER WHITE VERMOUTH

1 THIN STRIP LEMON PEEL, FOR GARNISH

Makes 1 drink

In a mixing glass, stir the whiskey and vermouth. Pour into a rocks glass filled with ice. Top with a lemon peel.

KIRA BIRNEY'S COFFEE LIQUEUR

From Caroline Bell, owner of
Cafe Grumpy and Coffee Roastery

Their logo may sport a frowny face, but happy are those coffee drinkers who live near one of Cafe Grumpy's two Brooklyn shops. Their carefully curated organic, fair-trade beans—including their seasonally changing Heartbreaker espresso blend and single-estate varietals you can order brewed by the cupful—are all roasted at their quiet corner café near the northernmost tip of Brooklyn. This recipe—where the aromatic notes of excellent coffee shine through the sweetness—comes from longtime barista Kira Birney, says owner Caroline Bell. "Every winter, she uses our coffee beans to make (and share) this delicious concoction," which is "awesome over vanilla ice cream or in a White Russian."

You may want to make this a month or so ahead of time, as time mellows the intense sweetness. The beans are available from *cafegrumpy.com*.

1 LB WHOLE CAFÉ GRUMPY
  HEARTBREAKER ESPRESSO
  BEANS OR YOUR FAVORITE
  ESPRESSO BLEND
6 TBSP VANILLA EXTRACT
5 CUPS VODKA
8 CUPS SUGAR IN THE RAW OR
  ANY TURBINADO SUGAR

4 CUPS WATER
PINCH OF SALT

SPECIAL EQUIPMENT:
10 (8 OZ) MASON JARS WITH
    TIGHTLY FITTING LIDS

Makes 10 (8-ounce) jars

1 In a large glass bottle tightly covered with cheesecloth, steep the coffee beans and vanilla in the vodka, unrefrigerated, for 1 month in a cool dark place.

2 Strain the liquid into a large stock pot and add the sugar, water, and salt. Bring to a boil over medium heat. Reduce the heat and let simmer for an hour, until the mixture begins to thicken but not caramelize. Stir occasionally to prevent the sugar from burning.

3 Let cool. Decant into Mason jars and seal tightly. The liqueur will be ready to drink immediately, but it will be very sweet. The sweetness will mellow over time, and the liqueur can be stored for up to a year, unrefrigerated, before serving.

KICK-ASS RED SANGRIA

*From Adam Goldstein of Red White &
Bubbly wine shop in Park Slope*

Adam Goldstein, owner of one of
Brooklyn's best wine shops in one of its
most refined neighborhoods, says that sangria shouldn't be fussy. The man may sell
one of the world's most complicated bev-
erages, but this sangria is anything but.
"Even most bad red sangrias are good," he
insists. The key is lots of fruit, plenty of
liquor, a bit of sweetness (delivered here
via orange juice and Sprite) and a rest in
the fridge to let the quaff come together.
Think this recipe looks a bit sloppy and
trashy? It's actually totally tasty, says
Goldstein, and perfect for a boozy summer party.

3 BOTTLES RED WINE, PREFERABLY
AN INEXPENSIVE MERLOT OR
TEMPRANILLO
1 BOTTLE BRANDY
1 BOTTLE TRIPLE SEC
1 (2-LITER) BOTTLE SPRITE
1 QT ORANGE JUICE
2 WHOLE APPLES, CORED AND CUT
INTO THIN WEDGES
2 WHOLE PEARS, CORED AND CUT
INTO THIN WEDGES
2 WHOLE ORANGES, CUT INTO
WEDGES
1 BUNCH GREEN OR RED SEEDLESS
GRAPES, STEMMED AND CUT
IN HALF
4 PLUMS, SEEDED AND CUT INTO
THIN WEDGES

Serves 15–20

1 Pour the wine into a large drink cooler with a spout on the bottom
(or use an extra-large stainless-steel stock pot). Pour in brandy from the
bottle by slowly counting to three. Pour in triple sec from the bottle
by slowly counting to three. Pour in Sprite from the bottle by slowly
counting to four.

2 Pour in orange juice, just until the red wine starts to become cloudy
(usually at the count of four or five, says Goldstein). Add the fruit and
let sit, covered, for a few hours, or refrigerate overnight. Ladle the fruit
and wine into glasses filled with ice, or serve the sangria on the rocks
and the fruit as a sangria-soaked fruit salad.

THE PRIME MEATS PEAR OLD-FASHIONED

*From Damon Boelte, bartender at
Prime Meats in Carroll Gardens*

As a mixologist behind the beautiful bespoke bar at Prime Meats, Damon Boelte makes some of the best cocktails in a community that counts many of the country's best bartenders as residents. Part of Boelte's charm as a drink maker is his willingness to tinker, and to make his own ingredients. Boelte's Barlett Pear Bitters, which are spiked with warming notes of cinnamon, clove, and allspice, were inspired by Prime Meats' backyard. Shared with Frankie's 457—whose chef-owners, Frank Falcinelli and Frank Castronovo, also run Prime Meats—it's the home of a Bartlett pear tree that sends out quantities of fruit every fall. Used sparingly—usually just a drop or two—to flavor the majority of classic drinks, bitters are made by aging a base spirit infused with various botanicals. Boelte replaces the traditional Angostura bitters with his own real house brand.

Edible Tip

Damon Boelte's Bartlett's Pear Bitters are happily now bottled in bulk and available nationally through *FranksPM. com*. Other varieties of pear bitters are scarce in the States, so as a substitute for Boelte's you could instead try a unique flavor made by a nationally distributed bitters company such as Fee's or Bitter Truth.

2 OZ RITTENHOUSE 100-PROOF RYE,
   OR USE ANOTHER RYE WHISKEY
¼ OZ SIMPLE SYRUP (PREFERABLY
   MADE WITH UNREFINED CANE
   OR TURBINADO SUGAR)
2–3 DROPS BARTLETT PEAR BITTERS

1 THIN STRIP LEMON PEEL,
   FOR GARNISH

Makes 1 drink

1 In a mixing class, stir the whiskey, syrup, and bitters over ice. Strain into a rocks glass filled with more ice. (Boelte recommends using one large chunk or cube to serve the drink, if possible.)

2 Top with the lemon peel.

PRIME MEATS

THE EGG CREAM

The sparkly-sweet drink that has been refreshing for more than a century.

There's a sign on the wall of the Brooklyn Farmacy & Soda Fountain, the new-fashioned shrine to retro soda jerkery in Carroll Gardens. It reads: "Pour ½ inch of cold whole milk into a tall, chilled, straight sided glass. Spoon in 2 tablespoons of chocolate syrup. Add bubbly seltzer to the top then stir vigorously with a long spoon to make a big, delicious, cold chocolaty drink. Enjoy!!"

Chocolate egg cream—the simple yet mythic refresher that's part of the collective soul of Brooklyn! Pete Freeman, co-owner of the Farmacy, is one of a new generation of jerks slinging seltzer to a new generation of drinkers. "The egg cream is like history," says Jen Albano, who co-owns the Cobble Hill bar Henry Public with her husband, Matt Dawson, and is raising their toddler on the egg cream the Farmacy serves. "It is an experience in a glass."

Yet unlike some old-time egg creamers, she's not overly doctrinaire on the subject. The owners of meccas like Gem Spa in the East Village would sooner sell out their mother than reveal the secrets to their frothy creations, and argue bitterly about the proper construction of the drink. They also tell you with a straight face that they make the best egg cream in the world,

whereas Freeman simply shrugs: "This is the best egg cream I can make."

"I've had a lot of people give me advice" says St. John Frizell, of Fort Defiance in Red Hook. "One person will say less syrup, more milk, or vice versa, or even speak to the order of ingredients."

Like the recipe, the history of the egg cream is, as Frizell puts it, "confusing." One yarn is that Yiddish stage star Boris Thomashevsky created the

drink after sampling a *chocolate et crème* in Paris, which, misprounced, became "chocolate egg cream." The most common tale lays authorship with Jewish candy-store owner Louis Auster, who opened a legendary shop on Second Avenue in the early twentieth century, though some report he'd gotten his start mixing sodas in Brooklyn.

"It seems like more a Brooklyn thing than a Manhattan thing." Frizell shrugs. "I always associate it with Brooklyn." Two big points in Brooklyn's favor: the chocolate syrup purists say make

the "true" egg cream—Fox's U-bet, made for the last century or so by H. Fox & Co.—is manufactured in Brownsville; and Canarsie is the home of the Gomberg Seltzer Works, a refilling plant that is the last of its kind on the East Coast to supply seltzermen like Ronny Beberman, who can be seen tooling around the borough, his 1950s truck covered with blue and green glass bottles still happily in use.

But Freeman switched from those after checking out the seltzer system at Fort Defiance. "It started with my love of seltzer," says Frizell. "I wanted it to be really bright, really sharp." So he found Ron Starman, an evangelistic third-generation seltzerman, to install his customized seltzer works. "Ron said, 'So, are you doing egg creams? You've got better seltzer than anyone else in the borough right now. It would be a crime not to do egg creams.'"

Freeman not only followed suit, but revived the Starman tradition of selling egg creams on the streets from a stainless-steel cart. "We get validation almost every day," said Freeman, "when you see someone sit down with their kid and say, 'We're going to have an egg cream!' I had a kid the other day. The mom was so fired up: she had her camera ready—his first egg cream."

FOX'S U-BET EGG CREAM

From Kelly Fox, executive vice president of H. Fox & Co., Inc., makers of U-bet chocolate syrup

There is little in the disputed history of the egg cream—New York's iconic drink that contains no egg and no cream—that locals agree on. But one thing is for certain: an authentic drink must be made with Brooklyn's very own Fox's U-bet chocolate syrup, made for five generations at H. Fox & Co., the family-run flavoring company. "The first time I ever made one was at a restaurant with my grandparents," says Kelly Fox, who now runs the century-old company.

Edible Idea

It's no wonder that where you find traditional egg creams you also find long pretzel sticks; odds are the marriage began when an egg-cream-slurping patron helped himself to the pretzel canister that sat on soda-shop counters all over Brooklyn (and New York City in general). It's still the most authentic way to enjoy this drink, so order an egg cream; grab a pretzel; slurp, dip, and crunch.

U-BET CHOCOLATE SYRUP
WHOLE MILK
SELTZER

Makes 1 egg cream

1 Spoon 1 inch of U-bet chocolate syrup into a tall, straight-sided 8-ounce glass. Add 1 inch of whole milk.

2 Pour in seltzer to just below the top of the glass. Stir gently, drink, and enjoy.

WARM SPICED GINGER TEA

Caroline Mak and Antonio Ramos,
co-owners of Brooklyn Soda Works

These hardworking food sellers run their incredibly bright and fresh-tasting from-scratch sodas—such as the superfresh berry-pink raspberry mint, a killer herry-Thai basil, or a spicy lemon and ginger—through CO_2 tanks, carbonating them on the spot. (The fruit and tea bases are crafted after hours in the kitchen of a local restaurant.) This particular tea "holds special significance for us," says Mak, "as this was one of the first drinks we made that we tried to carbonate and transform into a soda."

1 QT WATER
¾ CUP SLICED FRESH, PEELED
  GINGERROOT
1 PIECE STAR ANISE
5 CARDAMOM PODS
10 WHOLE CLOVES

JUICE FROM 1 LEMON
  (ABOUT 2 TBSP)
4 TBSP HONEY

Serves 4

1 Bring the water to a boil in a large pot. Add the gingerroot, star anise, and cardamom. Simmer for 20 minutes. Add the cloves and simmer for an additional 5 minutes. Turn off the heat, and add the lemon juice and the honey.

2 Strain out the spices and ginger and serve in mugs. You can also use more ginger for an increased spice level, or substitute orange juice for the lemon juice, adding a bit of orange zest along with the cloves.

THE PERFECT COLD BREW

From Darleen Scherer,
co-owner of Gorilla Coffee

In Brooklyn, a daily cup of iced coffee—served with a straw, of course—has become as much a summer ritual as a cone from the ice cream truck. Gorilla Coffee was one of the first to master the drink back in 2002. Their trick is simple: steeping the beans slowly over cold water, which "produces a naturally low-acid, full-bodied and smooth coffee concentrate that may be refrigerated for up to fourteen days without any deterioration in taste of freshness," says Darleen.

9 CUPS COLD OR ROOM-
  TEMPERATURE WATER,
  PREFERABLY FILTERED
1 LB GORILLA COFFEE BEANS,
  COARSELY GROUND

Makes 48 fluid oz (6 cups)
coffee concentrate

1 Pour 1 cup of water into a large pitcher, clean stock pot, or other brewing container. Add ½ pound of coffee, and pour 4 cups of water over the grounds, adding the water in a circular motion and making sure all the grounds get wet and there are no dry pockets. Add the remaining ½ pound of coffee. Slowly pour 3 additional cups of water over the grounds. Wait 5 minutes and slowly add 1 cup of water, without stirring. Ensure that all the grounds are wet by tapping the topmost grounds with the back of a spoon. Set aside to cold brew for 12 hours.

2 Pour the coffee concentrate through a filter into a pitcher and refrigerate. To make a cup of ice coffee, add water and ice to your taste in proportions of 1 part coffee to 1 part filtered water.

TONY'S TIRAMISU

From Tony Muia, owner of
A Slice of Brooklyn Bus Tours

Home to one of the bigger Italian American populations in the country, Brooklyn has always taken its pizza very seriously. And for more than twenty-five years Tony Muia, a Brooklyn native, has led hungry people to the tastiest pies in town . . . though which is best is always up for debate. Do you like crisp, thin crusts? There's the perpetually packed tourist haunt Grimaldi's under the Brooklyn Bridge. Is it thick squares of Sicilian-style pies? Then there's the block-long L&B Spumoni Gardens in Bensonhurst. And don't forget DiFara's in Midwood, whose owner Dominic DeMarco grows his own basil and orders his mozzarella from Italy and whose crusty, bubbly pies are without question some of the best in the world. No matter which you choose, however, you'll still need dessert, and Tony's got the answer: tiramisu. "It's so good," says Muia, "that I'm not allowed to go anywhere during the holidays, especially Christmas Eve, unless I bring my tiramisu with me."

10 EGG YOLKS
10 TBSP SUGAR
8 OZ MASCARPONE
2 TBSP SWEET MARSALA WINE
2 PT HEAVY CREAM
1 PACKAGE LADYFINGERS (OR SAVOIARDI IN ITALIAN)
10 CUPS STRONGLY BREWED ESPRESSO
UNSWEETENED COCOA POWDER, FOR DUSTING

Serves 12–15

1 Place the egg yolks and sugar in a large mixing bowl and, using a hand mixer, beat until the mixture turns bright yellow.

2 Add the mascarpone and gently beat into the egg yolk mixture until it's smooth and evenly mixed. Fold in the wine.

3 In a separate bowl, whip the heavy cream until it stands in stiff peaks. Gently fold the whipped cream into the egg yolk mixture and set aside.

4 Dip the ladyfingers into the espresso and lay them across the bottom of a 12-inch-long rectangular glass baking pan, 6 inches wide by 4 inches deep.

5 Ladle half of the cream mixture over the ladyfingers until it's about an inch thick. Repeat with the rest of the ladyfingers and cream mixture.

6 Sift a generous amount of unsweetened cocoa powder over the top of the tiramisu and refrigerate for several hours or overnight.

Edible Tip

When making tiramisu, it's important to use a glass baking pan, so that all the layers are visible when you serve.

CONCORD GRAPE ICE CREAM

From Kelly Geary,
founder of Sweet Deliverance

Without question, Kelly Geary is one of our favorite locavore entrepreneurs—the Natural Gourmet Cookery School grad caters Brooklyn rock shows; runs a food-delivery service that brings bacon-chive biscuits and squash gratin right to your door; markets a line of locally sourced jellies and jams; and even teaches how-tos to her neighbors in local classrooms. Those lucky enough to subscribe to her CSA-sourced meal plans (she picks up your share and turns it into great eats) often find pints of this remarkably simple frozen sweet in fall, which is made with the purple Concord grape found across the Northeast. "This ice cream is super-easy and has an awesome texture for not being made from a custard," says Geary. If you want to share it with friends, she suggests, "you can usually talk a restaurant out of three or four to-go soup containers with the cardboard lids to put your ice cream in."

2½ LB CONCORD GRAPES, WASHED AND PICKED CLEAN OF STEMS AND ANY BRUISED OR BROKEN FRUITS
1½ CUPS SUGAR
2½ CUPS HEAVY CREAM

SPECIAL EQUIPMENT:
ICE CREAM MAKER

Makes 3½ pints

1 Place the cleaned grapes in a medium-size saucepan with the sugar, and cook over medium-high heat, watching and stirring frequently, for 25–30 minutes, until the fruit has broken down. Let cool slightly.

2 Use a fine-mesh sieve to strain the mixture into a large heatproof bowl, pushing it through with a rubber spatula until there is nothing in the strainer but skins and seeds.

3 When you have everything pushed through, clean your spatula and scrape the grapes clinging to the underside of the strainer into the bowl. Repeat the process once or twice.

4 Combine the cream with the grapes and chill the mixture in the refrigerator overnight, or until very cold. Pour the mixture into an ice cream maker and churn until it looks like soft serve. Spoon the ice cream into a container and place in the freezer for a few hours or overnight.

Edible Tip

A cash crop for juice and jelly, beautifully blue-black Concord grapes are indigenous to the Northeast and are the essence of grapey goodness. One of the best Concord grape growers in the state is Brooklyn native Ken Farnan, of Buzzards Crest Vineyard. He now lives in the Finger Lakes but still brings nearly a dozen kinds of table grapes back home to sell at local farmers' markets.

MINT AND HONEY ICE CREAM

From Winnie Yang,
managing editor of The Art of Eating

A former editor for *Slow Food* who once spent a year in Italy working at their headquarters, Winnie Yang cures her own meats in her Brooklyn loft and hosts many food fests, including an annual BLT party for which she once made lettuce and tomato sorbets. Those were good, but this custardy summer concoction is even better. If you follow Yang's lead and use Cuisinart's ICE-50 ("It will change your life," she says), it'll be all the easier.

Edible Technique

This recipe lends itself to a multitude of variations: add in a cup of toasted coconut, one vanilla bean (the pod plus the insides scraped out) or one stick of cinnamon and two teaspoons dried instead of the fresh mint leaves. Or replace the honey with 2 tablespoons maple syrup or molasses, or ¼ cup sugar.

2 CUPS HEAVY CREAM
1 CUP WHOLE MILK
2 CUPS PACKED MINT LEAVES, WASHED AND DRIED
4 EGG YOLKS
¼ CUP SUGAR
¼ CUP HONEY
⅛ TSP SALT

SPECIAL EQUIPMENT:
ICE CREAM MAKER

Makes about 6 cups

1 Heat the cream and milk together in a saucepan over low heat. Remove from heat just before the mixture reaches a boil, add the mint, and steep for a least 1 hour.

2 Whisk together the egg yolks, sugar, and honey in a large bowl. Bring the milk and cream back up almost to a boil, then turn off the heat. Add half of the milk mixture to the egg mixture one large spoonful at a time, whisking constantly so as not to cook the eggs. Pour the egg mixture into the pot with the remaining milk mixture and heat over very low heat, whisking constantly, until the mixture coats the back of a spoon, about 5–10 minutes.

3 Chill overnight, then process in an ice-cream machine according to the manufacturer's directions. Place in the freezer for a few hours, or overnight, until firm.

4 Serve plain, with chocolate sauce, or with a fresh fruit topping.

CINNAMON NUT RUGELACH

*From Dorothy Cann Hamilton,
founder and CEO of
The French Culinary Institute*

Oddly enough, this recipe from the founder of one of the country's very best French culinary schools—launched with help from master chefs Jacques Pepin, Alain Sailhac, and Andre Soltner in 1984—isn't for pâté or pot-au-feu. Instead it's for an Eastern European (and now Brooklyn) classic sweet pastry—the nutty, cinnamon-sugar-filled crescents called rugelach. Growing up in Marine Park, young Hamilton's expansive dietary canon "was all ethnic," she remembers: crackly kaiser rolls; fifty-cent Lundy's pies; Ebinger's crumb cake (which sustained her mother during pregnancy); Brennan & Carr jus-dipped roast beef sandwiches; authentically undersize bagels; cardoon and eggplant from an Italian vegetable monger's truck; or Sunday suppers with her Czech grandmother, who washed vegetables at a Wall Street restaurant. This recipe is her mother's, who made them each holiday season. "It isn't Christmas," says Hamilton, "unless I make them!"

1 STICK UNSALTED BUTTER, AT ROOM TEMPERATURE
4 OZ BRICK CREAM CHEESE, AT ROOM TEMPERATURE
¼ CUP SOUR CREAM
1 CUP SIFTED FLOUR
10 ALMONDS OR WALNUTS, FINELY CHOPPED
SUGAR
GROUND CINNAMON, TO TASTE

Makes 16 rugelach

1 Blend together the butter, cream cheese, and sour cream in a large bowl using the tines of a fork. Add the flour gradually until you have a soft, but not sticky, dough. Form into a ball and wrap in plastic wrap. Refrigerate for several hours or overnight.

2 Preheat the oven to 375°F and lightly grease a cookie sheet. Roll out the dough on a lightly floured board to ¼-inch thickness. Mix the nuts together with sugar and cinnamon to taste.

3 Sprinkle the nut mixture over the dough and run a rolling pin lightly over the sugared nuts to embed them in the dough. Using a sharp knife, cut the dough into quarters. Cut each quarter into 4 triangles, making 16 triangles. Starting at their wide edge, roll up each one tightly until the small point is on top. Shape into crescents.

4 Place the crescents on the cookie sheet and bake for 12–15 minutes, until lightly browned. Serve at room temperature.

Edible Tip

Brooklyn is filled with long-standing restaurants, bakeries, and food shops that devout Brooklynites dream (and talk, constantly) about: Brennan & Carr, a roast beef sandwich-lover's haven, is still in existence and serving thousands of die-hard fans every day. Ebinger's Bakery, which closed in 1972, was known for its Blackout Cake, named for Brooklyn's wartime safety blackouts; and Lundy's, Sheepshead Bay's popular seafood restaurant, operated from the 1930s until it closed in the late 1970s (a newer version opened more recently and closed in 2007). Patrons still weep.

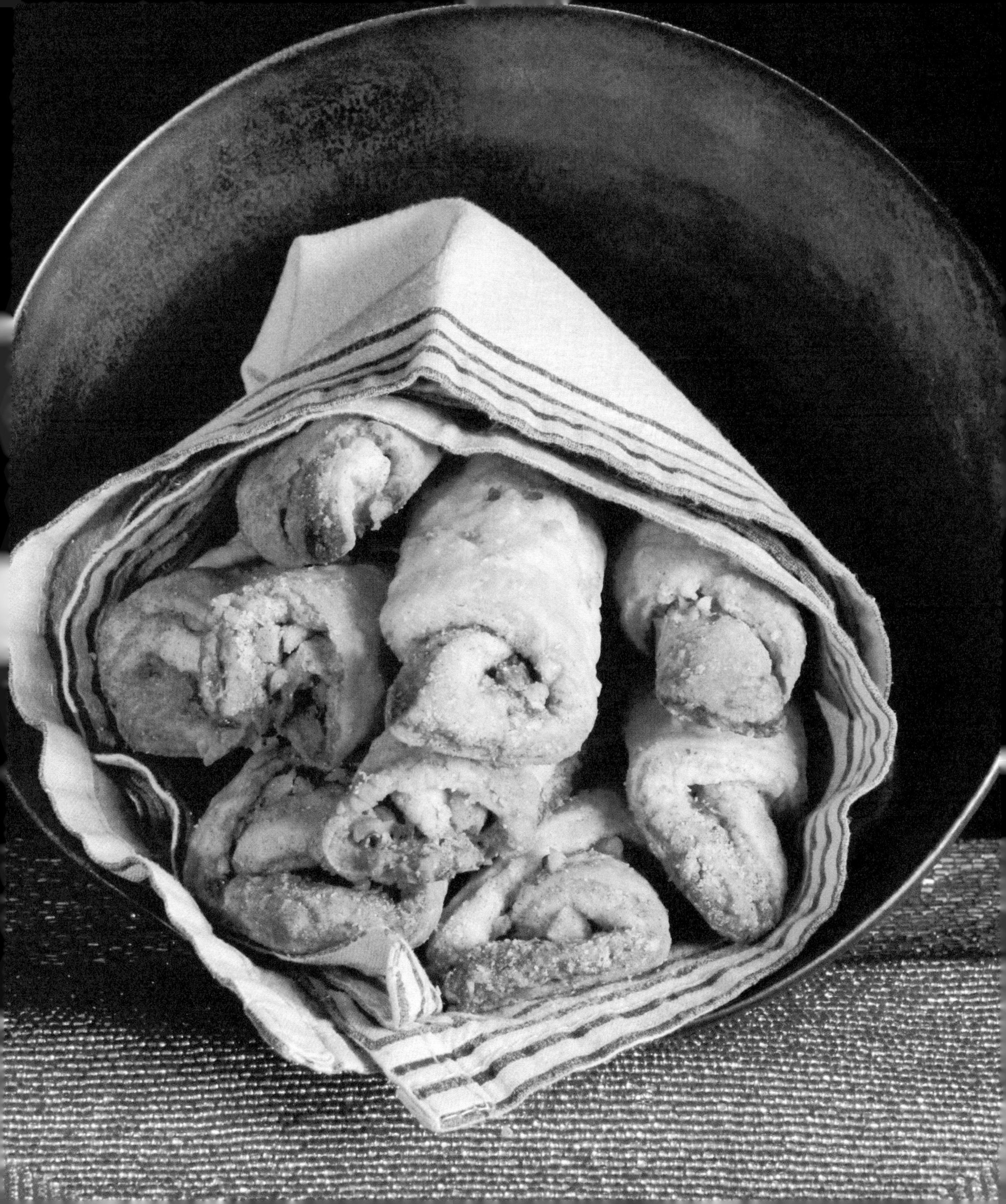

AUNT JANE'S STRAWBERRY PIE

*From Sara Matthews,
project manager, the urban farm at
Kingsborough Community College*

Sara Matthews helps run east Brooklyn's Kingsborough Community College urban farm and, not surprisingly, she knows her way around the seasons, adapting this strawberry pie to whatever tastes best or is in season at the time: "This is a fruit pie that my husband's grandmother used to make for her mother down in Virginia," she says. "I like to use seasonal fruit from the Grand Army Plaza greenmarket. In early summer I use strawberries; in mid-summer I use peaches, or two-thirds peaches with about one-third blueberries, or just blueberries." This pie is designed to be a bit runny, so bake it in the oven atop a cookie sheet to catch the spills as its juices flow over the side of the tin (which is how you'll know it's done). If you like your pie a bit on the tart side, reduce the amount of sugar the recipe calls for.

2   PREPARED 9-INCH PIECRUSTS
4–5 CUPS HULLED STRAWBERRIES,
    HALVED OR SLICED PEACHES,
    BLUEBERRIES, OR PEELED AND
    SLICED APPLES WITH A LITTLE
    CINNAMON IN THE FALL
1   CUP SUGAR

JUICE FROM ½ LEMON, STRAINED
    (ABOUT 1½ TBSP)
⅛   TSP SALT
2   HEAPING TBSP FLOUR
2   TBSP BUTTER

Makes 1 pie

1 Preheat the oven to 350°F, and place the bottom crust into a pie pan.

2 In a medium bowl, combine the fruit, sugar, lemon juice, salt, and flour and heap the mixture into the pie shell.

3 Dot the fruit mixture with butter and gently cover the pie with the second crust. Crimp the edges to seal. Using a sharp paring knife, make 5 (2-inch) slashes in the top of the piecrust to allow the steam to escape.

4 Place the pie in the oven on top of a cookie sheet to catch spills, and bake for 60–70 minutes. Keep an eye on the crust for the last 15 minutes to make sure it doesn't get too dark. If it starts to brown, cover the top loosely with aluminum foil. Once the juices begin to bubble out the sides of the tin, you'll know it's done.

5 Serve the pie warm, topped with a scoop of vanilla ice cream.

SPICEBUSH ICE CREAM

From Leda Meredith,
author of The Locavore's Handbook

When Brooklyn botanist and dancer Leda Meredith embarked on a yearlong challenge to eat foods sourced within 250 miles of her Brooklyn neighborhood, she started with farmers' markets, a nearby food co-op, her CSA, and her backyard. But with the magnificent 585-acre Prospect Park a short walk away—like Manhattan's Central Park, it was designed by Frederick Law Olmstead and Calvert Vaux in the 1800s—Meredith made a point to learn what grew there. She now leads foraging tours to help fellow locavores spot edibles from hearty burdock roots to delicate red clover blossoms. In this homemade ice cream—a creamy treat on its own, even in plain vanilla—Meredith uses the fragrant, peppery fall berries of spicebush (*Lindera benzoin*), a woodland shrub native to the northeastern states. You can order them from *IntegrationAcres.com* (they call it "Appalachian Allspice"), take one of Meredith's tours (*LedaMeredith.com*), or substitute allspice, cinnamon, and vanilla to re-create its woodsy allure. This ice cream is also especially delicious, says Meredith, made with the milk and honey available at the Saturday farmers' market at the base of the park.

1 PT HEAVY CREAM
½ CUP LOCAL HONEY
¼ TSP SALT
1 PT MILK
1 TSP GROUND SPICEBUSH BERRIES (GRIND THEM IN A COFFEE GRINDER), OR SUBSTITUTE ¼ TSP GROUND ALLSPICE PLUS ¼ TSP FRESHLY GROUNDED BLACK PEPPER PLUS ½ TSP GROUND CINNAMON

1 TSP VANILLA EXTRACT (OPTIONAL, IF YOU'RE KEEPING IT 100 PERCENT LOCAL)

Makes 1 quart

1 In a medium saucepan set over medium-low heat, bring 1 cup of the cream, the honey, and the salt to a simmer. Remove it from the heat and pour into a medium bowl.

2 Whisk in the remaining cup of cream, the milk, the ground spicebush, and the vanilla if using. Cover and refrigerate overnight or for as long as 24 hours.

3 Pour the mixture into an ice cream machine and process according to the manufacturer's instructions. Place in the freezer for a few hours, or overnight, until firm.

Edible Tip

Spicebush has teardrop-shaped leaves with smooth margins and a sharp, uneven point at the tip. The entire plant is aromatic, and the leaves, twigs, and bark make a wonderful tea. Small yellow flowers appear in early spring, and by fall, bright red oval berries a little less than a centimeter in length appear on the female shrubs. These are easily dried.

SALTED CARAMEL APPLES

*From Matt Lewis and Renato Poliafito,
co-founders of Baked*

Matt and Renato, a former producer and graphic designer, respectively, went beyond the ordinary brownie when they opened Baked, which specializes in a spectrum of amazingly good updated American desserts. (Think PB&J on a layer of crisped rice cereal, Coca Cola–cocoa Bundt cakes, and of course, brownies made with dark chocolate, homemade caramel, and a sprinkle of *fleur de sel*.) Now the pair owns two Bakeds and has produced their second cookbook, *Baked: Explorations in the Fall of 2010*. Fittingly, Matt tells us, "I would prefer to live in a land of perpetual fall. My house would be simple, but the kitchen would be large and the back door would open onto a field of Macoun apple trees. The Macoun apple is the best eatin' apple in a world of fine apples (mind you, it is not a great baking apple)," says Matt. "It is crisp and clean tasting with just a hint of carefully balanced sweetness, and it makes for a mind-blowing caramel apple."

Edible Tip

For caramel apples, say the owners of Baked, "it is easier to work with small to medium fruit. In addition, smaller caramel apples are easier to eat, and the ratio of caramel to apple is just right."

10–12 **CRISP MACOUNS OR OTHER SMALL-TO-MEDIUM APPLES MEANT FOR EATING FRESH, RATHER THAN BAKING**
2 **CUPS HEAVY CREAM**
½ **VANILLA BEAN**
2 **CUPS SUGAR**
½ **CUP LIGHT CORN SYRUP**
3 **TBSP UNSALTED BUTTER**
1 **TSP FLEUR DE SEL**
A FEW HANDFULS OF ICE

SPECIAL EQUIPMENT:
10–12 (7-INCH-LONG) WOODEN DOWELS, SHARPENED ON ONE END
CANDY THERMOMETER

Makes 10–12 apples

1 Wash and thoroughly dry the apples and remove the stems. Set the apples on parchment-lined baking sheets a few inches apart. Insert a small dowel about three-quarters of the way through each apple.

2 Place the cream in a small, heavy saucepan. Cut the vanilla bean in half lengthwise and, using the tip of the knife scrape the seeds of the bean into the cream. Add the bean to the cream and simmer over very low heat for 10 minutes. Do not let the mixture boil. Remove from the heat and pour the mixture through a fine-mesh sieve into a bowl to remove the bean and any other fibrous pieces. Return the vanilla cream to the pan. Add the sugar, corn syrup, butter, and half the fleur de sel, making sure the mixture doesn't splash onto the sides of the pan. Place the pan over very low heat and stir very gently until the sugar and salt are dissolved. Immediately increase the heat to medium-high and clip a candy thermometer to the side of the pot. Heat the caramel mixture, without stirring, to 245°F.

3 Meanwhile, put a few handfuls of ice in a medium bowl that is large enough to accommodate the pan with the caramel mixture. When the caramel mixture reaches 245°F (and stays there for at least 1 minute but doesn't increase), remove from the heat and place the pan on top of the ice for 30 seconds to slow the cooking. Remove the pan from the ice.

4 Tilt the pan toward you to create a big pool of caramel and, working fast, immediately begin dipping the apples in it. Dip each apple only once, and don't worry about coating it evenly or completely. Return the caramel-dipped apples to the baking sheet, sprinkle with the remaining fleur de sel, and refrigerate until the caramel is set, about 10 minutes.

CORNMEAL BUCKWHEAT POUND CAKE

From June Russell,
farm inspection manager, Greenmarket

An important part of June Russell's job with Greenmarket—the New York City farmers' market program that runs more than forty weekly outposts—is to help find new farms and even new crops, working to promote customer interest at the same time. One of her current passions is bringing local flours, once plentiful in the Northeast but now nearly nonexistent—back to New York State. While traveling the countryside to find farmers and millers, says Russell, "I have brought home a lot of grains and flour to work with." Russell's one of the best home cooks we know, and as a result, those who travel to her lovely garden apartment for supper are often treated to her tests of new products, which these days include this earthy, rustic pound cake—almost like a cross between cake and corn bread—made with some of the country's most flavorful freshly milled artisanal cornmeal, whole wheat, and buckwheat flour. The latter is "especially tricky to work with," says Russell, "because it lacks gluten and is stiff for baking. It has great flavor, though, and is rich in nutritional value, and seems to work best when it is blended with other grains. Freshly ground grains are the key to this recipe, as you will really taste the corn, buckwheat, and wheat."

2 STICKS UNSALTED BUTTER,
   AT ROOM TEMPERATURE
½ CUP CAKE FLOUR
½ CUP BUCKWHEAT FLOUR
1 CUP COARSE GROUND YELLOW
   CORNMEAL OR POLENTA
1 CUP UNREFINED BROWN
   CANE SUGAR
¼ TSP SALT
5 LARGE EGGS, BEATEN
1 TSP VANILLA EXTRACT

Makes 1 loaf

1 Preheat the oven to 325°F. Grease (use 1 tablespoon butter) and flour a 9 x 5 x 3-inch metal loaf pan.

2 Whisk the cake flour, buckwheat flour, and cornmeal in a medium bowl to blend.

3 Using an electric mixer, beat 2 sticks butter in a large bowl until light and fluffy. Gradually beat in the sugar, and then the salt. Slowly add the beaten eggs and vanilla. Add the dry ingredients to the wet in 3 additions, beating just to blend after each addition.

4 Transfer the batter to the greased loaf pan and bake until the cake is brown on top and a tester (a wooden skewer or toothpick) inserted into the center comes out clean, about 1¼ hours. Cool the cake in the pan for at least 15 minutes. Turn the cake out onto a rack and cool completely.

Edible Technique

Russell suggests using coarse cornmeal or polenta for this recipe instead of fine cornmeal, because the batter is wet for so long that it softens the grain but still provides the bread with some texture. She also uses unrefined brown cane sugar, "which adds," she says, "a surprising softness and depth."

DULCE DE LECHE CHEESECAKE

*From Joyce Quitasol, pastry chef
and co-owner of Joyce Bakeshop*

When Joyce and her bakers created this luscious *dulce de leche*–drenched cheesecake with a pecan crust, they were hoping to celebrate the cultural diversity of Brooklyn in pastry form. "One of my bakers comes from a Spanish background, and she loves anything with *dulce de leche*," says Quitasol. "I love anything with pecans, and New York City is home to some of the best cheesecake I know . . . so this is what we came up with." It's been a customer favorite at the bakeshop ever since. If your neighborhood specialty store doesn't stock tins of *dulce de leche*—made by reducing condensed milk—it's easy to make the thick, creamy-caramelly sauce at home. Just be sure to allow an extra day of prep time if you make your own.

Edible Technique

The silky sauce called *dulce de leche* is found canned anywhere Latin Americans shop but is easy to make at home, says Quitasol. Boil one 14-ounce can of condensed milk in a pot of water for 4 hours, making sure the can is completely covered with liquid. (Add more water as it evaporates.) Remove the can and cool completely before opening.

4 TBSP UNSALTED BUTTER, MELTED
¾ CUP GRAHAM CRACKER CRUMBS
3 TBSP SUGAR
¼ CUP FINELY CHOPPED TOASTED PECANS, PLUS EXTRA, FOR GARNISH
3 (8 OZ) PACKAGES CREAM CHEESE
1¼ CUPS LIGHT BROWN SUGAR

4 EGGS
2 TSP VANILLA EXTRACT
¼ TSP SALT
¼ CUP HEAVY CREAM
½ CUP *DULCE DE LECHE*, FOR DRIZZLING

Serves 12–14

1 Make the crust: preheat the oven to 350°F. Melt the butter in a small saucepan over medium-low heat, pour it into a bowl, and toss it together with the graham cracker crumbs, sugar, and ¼ cup pecans.

2 Press the mixture into a 9-inch springform pan and bake for 8–10 minutes, until light brown. Allow the crust to cool.

3 Make the filling: in a large bowl, beat the cream cheese until smooth (or use the paddle attachment of a standing mixer). Mix in the sugar and using a rubber spatula scrape the sides and bottom of the bowl well to reduce the lumps in your batter.

4 Blend in the eggs one at a time, scraping down the bowl after each addition. Add the vanilla, salt, and heavy cream. Mix until everything is incorporated well. Pour the batter into the cooled crust.

5 Prepare a water bath by filling a roasting pan halfway with warm water. Set the cheesecake into the water bath and cover the roasting pan with foil. Bake for about 1 hour. (To check the cheesecake for doneness, give the pan a little shake. A perfectly baked cheesecake will jiggle very slightly in the center.)

6 Transfer the cheesecake to a rack to cool completely, then chill it in the refrigerator for about 1 hour before removing it from the pan. Before serving, generously drizzle the cheesecake with *dulce de leche* and top with toasted pecans.

VANILLA-ALMOND TEA PANNA COTTA
WITH BLUEBERRY-BASIL COMPOTE

From Allison Robicelli,
co-founder of Robicelli's Cupcakes

Allison and Matt Robicelli—both Brooklyn natives and chefs—make cupcakes. These days that hardly seems special, but Robicelli's Cupcakes are a spectacular breed, filled with things like homemade guava paste or warm pears and gorgonzola cream. This dessert isn't a cupcake, but it is the dish that got them married. "When Matt and I met," says Allison, "we were instantly crazy about each other but were too chicken to say. Our roundabout method of wooing was inviting each other over for dinner and cooking elaborate dishes. I figured if I showed off my culinary prowess enough to a fellow chef, he'd eventually be impressed. It took six weeks of cooking these ridiculous four-star dishes until we started dating, and six weeks after that we were engaged."

Edible Idea

Think you don't have room to grow anything? "Basil is one of the only foods that anyone can successfully garden in a two-foot by two-foot Dyker Heights backyard," says Robicelli, who grew up in one of Brooklyn's Italian American neighborhoods. "It's the most quintessentially Brooklyn smell I can think of. It's a very unexpected flavor in dessert but goes beautifully with the tartness of blueberries."

2 CUPS HEAVY CREAM
1⅓ CUPS WHOLE MILK
½ CUP PLUS 4 TSP SUGAR
1 TBSP (1 ENVELOPE) PLAIN GELATIN
1 BAG FRENCH VANILLA–FLAVORED BLACK TEA
1 BAG ALMOND-FLAVORED BLACK TEA
9 LARGE LEAVES BASIL, 4 LEFT WHOLE, 5 CUT INTO CHIFFONADE
1 EGG WHITE, LIGHTLY BEATEN WITH 2 TBSP WATER
SUPERFINE SUGAR, FOR DUSTING
1 PINT FRESH BLUEBERRIES
⅓ CUP WATER
⅛ TSP KOSHER SALT
FRESHLY GROUND BLACK PEPPER

Serves 4

1 Combine the heavy cream, milk, and ¼ cup sugar in a saucepan and heat slowly until almost at a boil. Remove from heat and keep warm. Put the gelatin into a large bowl and stir in ¼ cup of the hot milk mixture, setting aside to soften.

2 Add the tea bags to the remainder of the milk mixture and let steep for 5 minutes. Remove the tea bags, squeezing to extract all the liquid. Slowly pour the milk mixture into the gelatin mixture, whisking constantly to incorporate fully. Divide the mixture equally among four ramekins.

3 Refrigerate for 30 minutes, or until the mixture just begins to thicken. Gently swirl a knife or chopstick through each ramekin to distribute the tea flavor. Cover with plastic wrap and refrigerate for at least 4 hours, until set.

4 Make the candied basil: using a pastry brush, lightly coat the top side of 4 whole basil leaves with egg white. Sprinkle the basil with the superfine sugar to coat. Let dry at room temperature for 1 hour.

5 Meanwhile, place the blueberries, water, ⅓ cup sugar, and salt in a small saucepan and cook over medium heat, stirring occasionally with a wooden spoon until the mixture just begins to bubble. Remove from the heat and stir in the slivered basil leaves and a few grinds of pepper to taste. Keep warm.

6 To serve, remove the panna cotta from the refrigerator. Carefully invert each ramekin onto a plate, running a butter knife around the rim of the ramekin. Top with the warm blueberry compote and a candied basil leaf.

NUNU CHOCOLATES CROP-TO-CUP ESPRESSO TRUFFLES

From Justine Pringle and Andy Laird, co-owners of Nunu Chocolates

Pardon the cliché, but this husband-and-wife team make sweet music together. We mean it literally: Andy is a musician and Justine went along on tours to sell his albums during shows, deciding she should offer some of her homemade chocolates at the same time. They proved just as successful as the tunes, and now the pair have opened a chocolaterie serving craft beer, wine, and coffee along with their incredibly beautiful dark chocolate confections, such as cashew caramel bark or Prosecco ganache truffles. The beans are from the Brooklyn-based Crop to Cup, whose espresso blends come from family farms and are also found in one of Nunu's best-selling truffles. "There's a floral quality to their beans that really comes out in the ganache," says Justine, "and at the shop we do a lot of chocolate-wine pairings. We serve this one with a Cabernet Sauvignon from the Stellenbosch region of South Africa."

10 OZ HEAVY WHIPPING CREAM
1 OZ ESPRESSO BEANS, ROUGHLY CRUSHED OR GROUND
19 OZ CHOCOLATE, BROKEN INTO SMALL PIECES
4 TBSP UNSALTED BUTTER
5¾ OZ INVERT SUGAR (A LIQUID SWEETENER)
1 CUP COCOA POWDER

Makes about 2 dozen truffles

1 In a medium saucepan set over medium-low heat, combine the cream and crushed espresso beans, and simmer slowly for 5–6 minutes. Remove from the heat and let sit for 10 minutes. Strain the espresso beans out of the cream.

2 In a large heatproof bowl combine the chocolate, butter, and invert sugar. Fold in the espresso cream and gently heat over a double boiler to melt. Whisk gently until completely combined and smooth. Let cool, and refrigerate the mixture overnight, or until set.

3 Pour the cocoa powder into a medium bowl. Using a melon baller, scoop out a ball of soft truffle filling, roll it in the cocoa powder until it is covered, and place it on a baking sheet. Continue the same process until you've used up the rest of the filling.

4 Chill the truffles on the baking sheet in the refrigerator. Serve at once, or store in an airtight container in the fridge for up to 2 days.

Edible Tip

This recipe works with any chocolate, but Nunu has found that 53% cacao chocolate works best as a balance with the espresso flavor imparted by the coffee. The invert sugar, a liquid sweetener used especially for candy making, is available at *KitchenKraft.com*.

CONCETTA DIPALO'S RICOTTA CHEESECAKE

From Lou DiPalo,
co-owner of DiPalo's Fine Foods

Lou DiPalo is the fourth generation of DiPalo's to run DiPalo's Fine Foods in Manhattan's Little Italy, where he's known for stocking some of the best Italian products in the city—especially cheeses such as the fresh mozzarella and ricotta the shop still makes a few times a day. But like many Italian Americans, the DiPalo family calls the Bensonhurst neighborhood of Brooklyn home, and this recipe for a true Italian-style cheesecake—rich with a bit of salty tang from the ricotta—is from Lou's grandmother Concetta, who once worked the counters at DiPalo too.

UNSALTED BUTTER, FOR GREASING
2 CUPS SUGAR
½ CUP CRUSHED ZWIEBACK
   COOKIES OR GRAHAM CRACKERS,
   PLUS EXTRA FOR GARNISH
3 LB FRESH RICOTTA

6 EGGS
1 TSP VANILLA
4 TSP ORANGE-BLOSSOM WATER
¾ CUP CREAM

Serves 12

1 Butter a 9-inch springform pan and preheat the oven to 350°F.

2 Mix ½ cup sugar and the crushed cookies in a small bowl, and evenly coat the bottom and sides of the buttered pan with the mixture.

3 In a large bowl, mix 1½ cups sugar and the ricotta, eggs, vanilla, orange-blossom water, and cream, and pour into the cookie-coated pan.

4 Sprinkle the top with crushed cookies and place the springform pan on the center oven rack with a cookie sheet below to catch leaks. Bake for 1 hour, or until the center no longer jiggles; it may crack slightly. Let cool, remove from pan, and serve at room temperature.

KOMBUCHA-SOAKED APPLE GALETTE

From Jessica Childs,
co-owner of Kombucha Brooklyn

With her husband, Eric, Jessica Childs bottles the vinegary "tea" made from a mushroomlike fungus called kombucha that legions of fans believe helps prevent colds and support good health. The pair have played around with their artisanal product, using its pleasant astringent tang in creative ways. Here it's used almost like a spirit to soak the sliced apples.

2 LARGE APPLES, PEELED, CORED,
   AND SLICED ⅛ INCH THICK
1 CUP STRAIGHT UP KOMBUCHA
¾ CUP WHOLE WHEAT PASTRY
   FLOUR
¾ CUP UNBLEACHED WHITE FLOUR
1 TBSP PLUS 2 TSP UNREFINED
   CANE SUGAR
¼ TSP PLUS ⅛ TSP GROUND
   CINNAMON
¼ TSP BAKING POWDER

⅛ TSP SEA SALT
⅓ CUP COCONUT OIL, SOFTENED
   TO ROOM TEMPERATURE
   (BUT NOT LIQUID)
1 TBSP PLUS ¾ TSP VANILLA
   EXTRACT
4 TBSP GRADE A MAPLE SYRUP
RASPBERRIES OR MINT, FOR
   GARNISH

Serves 6

1 In a large saucepan set over medium heat, simmer the apples and kombucha together until the apples are tender but not mushy. Strain the apples from the sauce, reserving both, and set aside.

2 In a large bowl, combine the flours, 1 tablespoon sugar, ¼ teaspoon cinnamon, baking powder, and sea salt. Use a whisk to make sure all ingredients are fully incorporated and there are no clumps.

3 Make a crater in the center of the flour mixture and add the coconut oil. Cut and blend the oil into the flour using a spatula or two dinner knives. Add ¾ teaspoon vanilla extract, 1 tablespoon ice-cold water, and 2 tablespoons maple syrup and mix with a wooden spoon. The dough will get clumpy, but don't break up the clumps. Continue to add ice-cold water, 1 tablespoon at a time, until the dough looks consistently moist, but not soaked.

4 Place the dough on plastic wrap, gather up the edges and twist them together to make a ball. Flatten to about 2 inches thick and place in the refrigerator for 15 minutes.

5 Put an oven rack in the middle of the oven. Preheat the oven to 375°F. Remove the dough from refrigerator and let rest, wrapped, for 10 minutes.

6 In a bowl, mix together 2 teaspoons of cane sugar, ⅛ teaspoon cinnamon, and 1 tablespoon vanilla, add the apples, and toss until coated.

7 Unwrap the dough and dust it with flour. Stretch the dough out with your hands a bit, dust again with flour so that there are no wet pieces, and then roll between 2 pieces of parchment paper until the circle is about 9½ inches and of uniform thickness. If cracks appear in the center, work in a little ice-cold water to the area with your fingers, join the crack, and roll the dough out again. If the dough starts to get too sticky, dust with more flour.

8 Place the dough in the parchment paper on a sheet pan, and remove the top sheet of parchment. Fan the kombucha-spiked, cinnamon-coated apple slices in concentric circles on the dough, leaving a 1½-inch border around the edge and saving the most attractive slices for the top layer.

9 Fold the outer 1½-inch edge of the dough up and over the apples, leaving a large hole in the center so that the fanned apples show through. Cut the bottom layer of parchment paper, leaving an inch or so margin around the bottom crust, and refrigerate for 15 minutes.

10 Bake the galette in the middle of the oven for 25 minutes. Brush the pastry with a mixture of 2 tablespoons maple syrup and 2 tablespoons water and bake 5 minutes more. The crust should be brown and firm to the touch. Transfer to a rack to cool and serve garnished with the raspberries or mint.

AUTUMN PLATE-LICKER CAKE

From Anna Gordon,
founder of The Good Batch

One of many artisanal food makers at the outdoor market called the Brooklyn Flea (see profile, page 74) Anna Gordon is the only one thus far to base her bakery on Brooklyn history: The Good Batch specializes in *stroopwafels*, crispy paper-thin Christmas waffles eaten by the Dutch, our first settlers way back in 1634. (The village of Breuckelen, in fact, was named for a city in the Netherlands and in 1646 became the first official municipality in what is now New York State.) But Gordon is also known for plenty of other specialty sweets, like this wonderful whiskey-and-spiced-cider layer cake, made for a wedding and aptly named. "The challenge was that the groom did not like cake," Gordon tells us, "but he loved apple cider doughnuts . . . and bourbon. Although there might not have been any plate licking at that wedding, I have witnessed the act on several other, less formal occasions at which I have served the cake." Gordon gets her cider from a local farmers' market stand and suggests you do the same for maximum apple flavor.

½ CUP UNREFINED CANE SUGAR
1½ CUPS APPLE CIDER, AT ROOM TEMPERATURE
8 TBSP BOURBON
3½ STICKS BUTTER, AT ROOM TEMPERATURE, PLUS EXTRA FOR GREASING THE PANS
4 CUPS FLOUR
1 TBSP PLUS 1 TSP BAKING POWDER
1 TSP BAKING SODA
1⅛ TSP SALT
2 TSP GROUND CINNAMON
1 TSP GROUND GINGER
½ TSP GRATED NUTMEG
¼ TSP GROUND CLOVES
¼ TSP GROUND CORIANDER
6 EGG WHITES, AT ROOM TEMPERATURE
1 TBSP VANILLA EXTRACT
1½ CUPS WHITE SUGAR
12 OZ CREAM CHEESE, AT ROOM TEMPERATURE
2½ CUPS POWDERED SUGAR
JUICE FROM 1 LEMON

Serves 8–10

1 Make the syrup: in a small saucepan, stir together the unrefined cane sugar and ½ cup water. Bring to a boil, reduce to a simmer, and cook until the sugar has dissolved, about 4 minutes. Add ¼ cup apple cider and 2 tablespoons bourbon, and cook for 4 more minutes. Set aside, and let the syrup cool completely before using.

2 Position the oven racks in top and bottom third of oven and preheat the oven to 350°F. Coat the inside of two 9-inch cake pans with butter or cooking spray and line the bottom with parchment-paper circles. Butter or spray the parchment as well.

3 Sift together the flour, baking powder, baking soda, 1 teaspoon salt, and the spices in a bowl and set aside.

4 Combine the egg whites, vanilla, and ¼ cup apple cider and set aside.

5 With an electric mixer, beat 2 sticks softened butter for 1 minute in a large bowl. Add the white sugar and beat until light and fluffy, 3–4 minutes. Scrape down the bowl. While the mixer is on low, slowly pour in the egg white mixture. Continue mixing until the ingredients are fully incorporated. Scrape down the bowl.

6 Add the flour mixture and 1 cup cider to the batter in three additions, beginning and ending with the flour mixture. Scrape down the sides and the bottom of the bowl between additions.

7 Divide the batter evenly between the two pans. Tap the pans to release any air bubbles and wipe any dripped batter from the sides of the pan.

8 Put the pans on separate racks in the oven and bake for 30–40 minutes, switching pans halfway through. Remove from the oven and let cool completely.

9 Make the frosting: with an electric mixer, beat the cream cheese and 1½ sticks butter together until smooth and fluffy. Scrape down the sides of the bowl and add half the powdered sugar. Mix on low, scrape down the bowl, and add the remaining powdered sugar and ⅛ teaspoon salt. Beat on medium speed until fully incorporated. Add the lemon juice and 4 tablespoons bourbon and continue mixing. Add more bourbon if needed.

10 If your cakes have a dome shape, cut off the top so each layer is perfectly flat. Then cut each layer in half horizontally with a large serrated knife. Place the bottom layer on a cake board or plate and, using a pastry brush or spoon, thoroughly wet the top with the syrup. The cake should be moist but not soaking. Add a dollop of the frosting and spread evenly to create a ¼-inch-thick layer. Place the next cake layer on the frosting and repeat until all four layers have been stacked and filled.

11 Finish by frosting the cake as desired: either left open on the sides or fully covered.

BROOKLYN-MADE FOODS:
A LIST OF BROOKLYN SHOPS THAT DELIVER

BIERKRAFT One of the best beer stores in New York City—if not the country—Bierkraft sells hundreds of hard-to-find craft beers (and pours them as pints, too). Better still, they'll ship much of what they stock, including occasional bottles from Brooklyn's three breweries. *Bierkraft.com*

BROOKLYN LARDER This specialty food shop from the owners of Franny's, one of Brooklyn's best modern pizzerias and Italian restaurants, has its own cheese room, as well as shelves holding an excellent selection of pickles, jams, granola, chocolates, and other artisanal foods from Brooklyn, New York State, and beyond. *BklynLarder.com*

BROOKLYN OENOLOGY Owner Alie Shaper buys, ferments, and bottles her grapes on Long Island— the landmass Brooklyn shares with its eastern neighbor—offering samples of creations (whose labels are often drawn by local artists) in her Williamsburg tasting room, which features foods made in the borough. *BrooklynOenology.com*

BROOKLYN WINE EXCHANGE This modern Brooklyn wine shop focuses on wines made in small, sustainable production by family businesses. One of the most boutique brands they offer is Brooklyn's own Red Hook Winery, just a few miles away. *BrooklynWineExchange.com*

GILLIE'S COFFEE Brooklyn is now home to a handful of small, incredible coffee roasters that provide online shipping—check out *GorillaCoffee.com, CafeGrumpy.com, OsloCoffee.com*—but the oldest is Gillie's, which has been roasting beans since 1840. *GilliesCoffee.com*

HERITAGE FOODS USA Launched by one of Slow Food USA's founders to help support their efforts to save American food traditions, this Brooklyn-based organization is a national source for some of the country's very best sustainably raised, heritage-breed meats from small family farms, as well as other American heritage products such as grains, honey, and spices. *HeritageFoodsUSA.com*

JUNIOR'S A literal Brooklyn landmark, this downtown Brooklyn diner is famous for its brilliant neon sign and its ultrarich cheesecake, which comes in multiple flavors, all shipped nearly anywhere in the famous bright-orange striped box. *JuniorsCheesecake.com*

LANDI'S PORK STORE One of Brooklyn's many long-standing pork stores—or Italian butcher shops— Landi's is a source for superb fresh pork sausages from broccoli rabe to parsley and cheese as well as dried, cured links such as sopressata and pepperoni. They also ship a treasure trove of Italian American treats including mozzarella, meat sauce, and chicken parm. *BrooklynPorkStore.com*

BROOKLYN LARDER, PROSPECT HEIGHTS

THE KING OF CHEESES!

G. CRAVERO

SINCE 1855

PARMIGIANO REGGIANO

HAND SELECTED & AGED BY GIORGIO CRAVERO
IN BRA-PIEDMONT, ITALY

HAND-CRAFTED AT LATTERIA #2967
DELLA CROCE BENEDELLO IN
PAVULLO NEL FRIGNANO VILLAGE
(JUST OUTSIDE MODENA IN EMILIA-ROMAGNA)
FROM THE MILK OF COWS THAT PASTURE
IN THE APPENINE HILLS AT THE
ALTITUDE OF 2300 FEET.

MILL BASIN KOSHER DELICATESSEN If it's authentic Brooklyn Jewish deli you're after—latkes, chopped liver, noodle kugel, and matzo ball soup—head to Mill Basin Kosher Delicatessen on Avenue T. Luckily for those who live outside of the borough, they'll ship their fatty, smoky pastrami, brisket, and corned beef. *Pastrami.net*

STINKY BKLYN One of the borough's better shops for cured meats and American and European cheeses, this small specialty foods shop also sports a lengthy list of locally made products, including the pickles, kimchi, soda, coffee, and chocolate-stuffed "Brooklyn sampler," which we believe is the perfect gift. *StinkyBklyn.com*

THE BROOKLYN KITCHEN / THE MEAT HOOK A well-stocked kitchenware store, culinary classroom, world-class butcher shop, and specialty foods market that will ship many of the Brooklyn-made pickles, sweets, sauces, coffee, jams, and other products it stocks, from kraut crocks and home-brew supplies to seltzer systems, as well as hard-to-find spices and extracts. *TheBrooklynKitchen.com*

PASTOSA RAVIOLI This fresh pasta maker ships more than its namesake pasta pillows—which come in a nearly a dozen varieties—including manicotti, stuffed shells, lasagna, tortellini, red sauce, sausages, and, last but not least, their famous handmade fresh mozzarella. *Pastosa.com*

BROOKLYN BOOKS AND WEBSITES

What to read if you want to truly know Brooklyn food (besides *Edible Brooklyn,* that is).

BROOKLYN: A STATE OF MIND This compendium of 125 stories from "America's Most Colorful City"—we agree!—includes not just great moments in borough history and the changing makeup of its multifaceted communities, but also a great deal of food lore. Nathan's hot dogs, Junior's cheesecakes, fishing off the piers, and Brooklyn beer? Yep. Old-fashioned Brooklyn potlucks and literary breakfast clubs? Those are in here too. Michael W. Robbins and Wendy Palitz (Workman, 2001).

BROOKLYNBASED.NET We love this site. While its well-researched and ahead-of-the-curve electronic missives aren't always about food, they are written by and for cool Brooklynites with a passion for getting to know their city and how to best support it, a sentiment of which we highly approve.

BROOKLYNPAPER.COM Printed each Friday, *The Brooklyn Paper* is also available online, where archives of its boroughwide culinary news coverage and restaurant reviews have recently been augmented with a food-gossip blog revealing the location of the latest artisanal pickle, new taco truck, or authentic bagel.

BROOKLYN-USA.ORG There is likely no bigger booster for Brooklyn than borough president, Marty Markowitz, a man so full of personality he scored a multipage profile in *The New Yorker*. He's a native with a penchant for Brooklyn's storied past and its plentiful places to eat, and his official website has plenty of news about dining habits new and old, as well as links to his newsletters—which we look forward to each month for the excellent profiles of little-known restaurants and cooks.

EDIBLEBROOKLYN.COM and *EDIBLECOMMUNITIES. COM* Beyond the printed pages of our quarterly magazine, *Edible Brooklyn* also lives online, and our site is home to borough food news, updates on the incredible people we cover, and extensive listings of Brooklyn food events and happenings we either host or want to attend. (You can also, of course, subscribe.) By the same token, you can subscribe, connect, and keep up with the nearly seventy Edible publications nationwide on Edible Community's site.

FOODCURATED.COM Video goddess Liza de Guia doesn't always stay in her home borough of Brooklyn, but her excellent short films about the making of our food—recently nominated for a James Beard Foundation Journalism award—are what we like to watch.

FOOD LOVER'S GUIDE TO BROOKLYN This almost-pocket-size guide is a great handbook to both haute eateries and the excellent holes-in-the-wall found boroughwide, plus grocery stores, farmers' markets, and food stalls. Want to know where to go for foie gras, Vietnamese pho, Armenian breads, or Trinidadian doubles? This is the book. Sherri Eisenberg (Globe Pequot Press, 2010).

THELMAGAZINE.COM Named after the Brooklyn-centric subway line that connects the superchic Brooklyn neighborhood of Williamsburg with downtown Manhattan, *The L Magazine* has since expanded to cover all of New York City, but Brooklyn life—young and hip Brooklyn life, that is—is still its main beat.

THE NEIGHBORHOODS OF BROOKLYN Brooklyn isn't so much a melting pot as a multiculti mix of neighborhoods with their own spirit, supermarkets, yearly festivals, and iconic foods. With an introduction by Kenneth Jackson—whose recent update of *The Encyclopedia of New York City* is also

worth a read for curious foodies—this book is your guide to the borough's many little city-states. John T. Manbeck and Kenneth Jackson (Yale University Press, 2004).

THE NEW BROOKLYN COOKBOOK In addition to recipes and stories from the thirty-one very best contemporary restaurants in a borough with some of the world's best food—as well as beautiful photography from *Edible Brooklyn* photo editor Michael Harlan Turkell—we love *The New Brooklyn Cookbook* for its sources list, a compendium of CSAs, farmers' markets, breweries, bars, wine shops, restaurants, specialty food markets, artisanal producers, and food trucks. Melissa Vaughan and Brendan Vaughan (William Morrow, 2010).

THE BROOKLYN COOKBOOK An incredible collection of recipes and recollections about Brooklyn's collective food culture, starting with the Lenape Indians and the Dutch and moving through the Italians and Irish to the West Indians and Syrian Jews. This richly layered book tells the stories of those who cook and eat in the borough throughout its history, from the oysters in the Gowanus Canal to the famous Blackout Cake made by now shuttered Ebinger's German bakery. Lyn Stallworth and Rod Kennedy Jr. (Knopf, 1991).

WALKING BROOKLYN You can take a taxi to Williamsburg's restaurant rows or the F subway line to Smith Street's eateries in Carroll Gardens, but the best way to experience Brooklyn food is by wandering its streets. Window-shop the Italian American market storefronts in Bensonhurst, stroll the Caribbean stalls in Crown Heights, meander from one end of Sunset Park (that's Chinatown) to the other (where countless Latin Americans live and eat). This book of historical and cultural tours will get you started off on the right foot. Adrienne Onofri (Wilderness Press, 2007).

ACKNOWLEDGMENTS

Edible Communities would like to thank our co-founder, Carole Topalian, for the elegant, compelling images that grace these pages; Rachel Wharton for hunting and gathering and editing the recipes and profiles for the book from throughout the Brooklyn community; Kelly Day, whose incredible organizational skills keep the Edible world rolling smoothly from one day to the next; and Elissa Altman, our indefatigable managing editor, who pulled it all together and somehow got all of us to make the shortest book deadline in history. To our grace-under-pressure recipe testers and stylists, particularly Michael Nicola and Tracey Ryder, we send our heartfelt thanks and gratitude. And to Stephen Munshin and Brian Halweil, publishers of *Edible Brooklyn*, we applaud your heroic effort—in Brooklyn, Manhattan, and the East End—to bring all things Edible to the readers and eaters of those communities. We would also like to thank our agent, Lisa Ekus, for her ongoing support for all we do—books and otherwise—and to the team at Sterling Publishing, our enthusiastic thanks for your vision and excitement toward our newly forged partnership, especially Carlo DeVito, Diane Abrams, Chris Thompson, Leigh Ann Ambrosi, and Blanca Oliveri.

Edible Brooklyn would like to thank, for starters, every one of the two hundred or so Brooklyn cooks, picklers, gardeners, farmers, bakers, butchers, activists, writers, artists, beekeepers, mozzarella makers, shopkeepers, cheesemongers, and other artisans we initially reached out to for

recipes, both those who made it into these pages and those who had to be left out because, well, we ran out of room. It's a testament to your collective force that Brooklyn food feels like a tightly knit community, rather than many individuals in isolated kitchens cooking away in one of the biggest cities in the world.

We'd also like to express our eternal gratitude to all of our supporters and advertisers, the Brooklyn businesses and businesspeople who help to keep our little quarterly magazine and its projects afloat. That goes as well to our contributing writers and photographers Amber Benham, Jeanne Hodesh, Scarlett Lindeman, Ben Schmerler, Robert Simonson, and David Wondrich—who were willing to contribute profiles to this book as a labor of love.

And we offer our greatest appreciation, admiration, respect, and love for the team that brings our magazine to life year after year, first and foremost the incredible force of nature that is Gabrielle Langholtz, our editor in chief and the person truly responsible for the success of its pages, who also gave greatly of her time to make this cookbook a reality. That also includes Michael Harlan Turkell, our photo editor, Katie Sweetman, our graphic designer, Samantha Seier, our events director, and Jeanne Hodesh and Amber Benham, our editorial assistants, without whom this cookbook would not have happened. An extra-special thanks to Amber, who spent many wee hours writing headnotes and tracking down missing ingredients.

PROFILE CREDITS

Page 4, Profile: Ian Cheney, Truck Farmer, was written by Jeanne Hodesh, the publicity coordinator for Greenmarket, the New York City farmers' market program, and *Edible Brooklyn*'s editorial assistant.

Page 10, Profile: Caroline Fidanza, Co-owner of Saltie, was written by Rachel Wharton, *Edible Brooklyn*'s deputy editor.

Page 31, Profile: The Tortilla Triangle was written by Scarlett Lindeman, a freelance writer, professional cook, and wannabe food historian with a master's degree in food studies from New York University.

Page 42, Profile: The Brooklyn Kitchen was written by Rachel Wharton, *Edible Brooklyn*'s deputy editor.

Page 66, Profile: Brooklyn Brewery was written by Rachel Wharton, *Edible Brooklyn*'s deputy editor.

Page 74, Profile: The Brooklyn Flea was written by Amber Benham, a former editorial assistant for *Edible Brooklyn* and a *Saveur* intern. She is a graduate of CUNY's master's program in journalism. Her specialty is multimedia reporting and storytelling, but she's also an excellent baker and speaks fluent Spanish, which she put to use during a yearlong stay in Spain.

Page 90, Profile: Mozzarella: The Way of the Curds was written by Benjamin Schmerler, a partner in First Press, a public relations and consulting company geared toward businesses in the food and beverage world.

Page 97, Profile: Franny's Pizza was written by Rachel Wharton, *Edible Brooklyn*'s deputy editor.

Page 112, Profile: The Brooklyn was written by David Wondrich, a cocktail historian and author of several books on drinks, including *Imbibe!* and *Punch.*

Page 122, Profile: The Egg Cream was written by Robert Simonsen, who writes about cocktails, spirits, wine, and beer for the *New York Times, Wine Enthusiast,* and others.